P9-DNU-771

The Knitting Way

A Guide to Spiritual Self-Discovery

LINDA SKOLNIK & JANICE MACDANIELS

Walking Together, Finding the Way
SKYLIGHT PATHS Publishing
Woodstock, Vermont

The Knitting Way:
A Guide to Spiritual Self-Discovery

2005 First Printing
© 2005 by Linda Skolnik and Janice MacDaniels

All rights reserved. No part of this book may be reproduced or transmitted in any form or by any means, electronic or mechanical, including photocopying, recording, or by any information storage and retrieval system, without permission in writing from the publisher.

For information regarding permission to reprint material from this book, please mail or fax your request in writing to SkyLight Paths Publishing, Permissions Department, at the address / fax number listed below, or e-mail your request to permission@skylight paths.com.

All photos courtesy of Marvin Skolnik.
Illustrations on pp. 9 and 13 courtesy of Jared MacDaniels.
Charts on pp. 47, 48, 65, 67, 208, and 209 created with *Stitch & Motif Maker,* Knitting Software, Inc.

Library of Congress Cataloging-in-Publication Data
Skolnik, Linda.
The knitting way : a guide to spiritual self-discovery/ Linda Skolnik and Janice Macdaniels.
    p. cm.
Includes bibliographical references.
ISBN 1-59473-079-2 (pbk.)
1. Knitting. I. MacDaniels, Janice. II. Title.

TT820.S528 2005
746.43'2—dc22

2005003155

10 9 8 7 6 5 4 3 2 1

SkyLight Paths Publishing is creating a place where people of different spiritual traditions come together for challenge and inspiration, a place where we can help each other understand the mystery that lies at the heart of our existence.
SkyLight Paths sees both believers and seekers as a community that increasingly transcends traditional boundaries of religion and denomination—people wanting to learn from each other, *walking together, finding the way.*

Manufactured in the United States of America
Cover Design: Sara Dismukes
SkyLight Paths, "Walking Together, Finding the Way," and colophon are trademarks of LongHill Partners, Inc., registered in the U.S. Patent and Trademark Office.

Walking Together, Finding the Way
Published by SkyLight Paths Publishing
A Division of LongHill Partners, Inc.
Sunset Farm Offices, Route 4, P.O. Box 237
Woodstock, VT 05091
Tel: (802) 457-4000   Fax: (802) 457-4004
www.skylightpaths.com

To all the knitters, and others with enthusiasm for learning, who feel a longing for connection and a thirst for meaning.

—L. S.

To all knitting souls who seek the knowledge and wisdom of the Holy and the deeper places of their spirits.

—J. M.

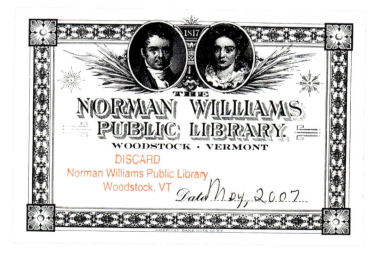

1817

THE
NORMAN WILLIAMS
PUBLIC LIBRARY
WOODSTOCK · VERMONT
DISCARD
Norman Williams Public Library
Woodstock, VT
Date May, 2007

AMERICAN BANK NOTE CO NY

Contents

Index of Patterns

Preface

The Knitting Way is what came from the convergence of the knitting journeys of two women from very different backgrounds, whose paths first crossed and mingled at a Yarn Paradise. That's the "way" of the Knitting Way. Connection happens through knitting. Now, as your path crosses ours, we invite and welcome you to come along. That's really why we wrote the book.

So, where did we begin? Linda, an only child, was born and raised in a small apartment (where she says she believed water came from the superintendent and vegetables came from the vegetable store) in the Flatbush section of Brooklyn, which was a Jewish Camelot. Although her family was not religiously observant, she always felt a connection to her heritage and traditions as a Jew. After IBM hired her husband, they moved to Poughkeepsie, New York, with their two children in 1969. Ten years later she began Patternworks, without which this book would not have been written. And if she had not sold Patternworks in 2002, looking forward to more time with her three grandchildren, this book still would not have been written. So, it seems, a full cycle had to be completed.

At another time, Janice was born in Illinois, the eldest of five children. Her early life took her from Illinois to Florida, with stops in Oklahoma, Wyoming, California, and Texas (twice) in between. This young family of seven eventually stopped moving. She grew up in Florida, her later childhood spent on the beach and in a boat, with strong cultural ties to the Midwest and farms, steeped in church and Sunday school Christianity. Marriage and IBM brought Janice and her husband to New York thirty years ago and now, with four children and two grandchildren, she says she still bears those ties with a little bit of the Northeast thrown in.

This book is about seeing and listening. It's about becoming aware that through knitting you can hear and give attention to what's in your heart and soul—that knitting can be a place of rest and thought and a place for the Divine. It's about connection—to yourself, to the world, to others, and to the Holy. You will find accounts of the Monday night discussions between us as we wrote the book and our explorations in between. You will meet other knitters and learn their stories. You will find thought-provoking patterns that were meant to be exercises to increase awareness and point to a spiritual and community connection. They also turned out to be lots of fun, because fun and play are part of the journey. You will find a place to add to the connection at www.theknittingway.com.

Linda serves as the voice of the story and Janice invokes the wonder of knitting and living in interludes identified as "Space between the Loops." You are encouraged to become a coauthor with us, to join in our journey as you live with this book. Use it as a kind of journal; write in the margins and mark it up. Take what you find and make it yours. Add to it. Make it work better for you. It was written to help you gain a little more—and a little deeper—sense of the mysterious and divine place in your soul through your knitting, as you join with kindred spirits on the Knitting Way.

Introduction

Finding the Knitting Way

Strange how this all started. I would never have thought twenty-five years ago when I started a mail-order business called Patternworks that it would lead me to find the Knitting Way.

I owned Patternworks from 1979 to 2002. The business I birthed and nurtured in my basement took on a life of its own, and we went together on a magic carpet ride as Patternworks became what Barbara Albright in *Knitter's Stash: Favorite Patterns from America's Yarn Shops* called "one of America's best-known knitting shops/warehouses/catalog companies ... a mecca ... for knitters from all over the world who come to revel in its vast selection of yarn and accessories."[1] I had married when I was a junior in college, working toward a BA (read: Mrs.) degree in psychology at Brooklyn College. My son, Daniel, was born a month after I graduated and my daughter, Karen, two years later. Predating the baby boom generation by a couple of years, I hadn't considered pursuing a career path. As the children became more self-sufficient, I was inspired to develop a business from home. Wracking my brain for a business idea, I took the spiritual advice of Russell Conwell in his classic self-help book *Acres of Diamonds* and focused on what was right in front of my eyes, which turned out to be my own yarn basket. I had loved to knit from the time my grandmother taught me the craft as a child. What could be better than turning a passion into a business?

If you were a knitting enthusiast back in the early 1980s, perhaps you remember Patternworks's early black-and-white leaflets called Hard-to-Find Things for Knitters. I loved every aspect of the little business—finding and developing gadgets and patterns, presenting them in a catalog, preparing ads and publicity, and supplying customers through the mail from my basement. The business slowly grew. Unfortunately, my marriage didn't survive.

By the time I married Marvin Skolnik in 1984, my beloved Patternworks had a few thousand devoted customers, although for an actual salary I worked in a yarn store. When Marvin took early retirement from IBM, he persuaded me to step outside my comfort zone and (1) get a toll-free phone number and (2) print the catalog in color (to sell yarn to knitters, duh). These steps worked so well that the business began taking over our small townhouse room by room until there was barely space for living. It's a wonder that the daily arrival of an employee, strenuous UPS exchanges, and the occasional tractor-trailer truck delivery didn't get us into hot water with the neighbors before we took the big plunge and rented a commercial space.

General interest in knitting declined from the mid-1980s through the mid-1990s, forcing mills and yarn stores to close in droves, but it was the right time for Patternworks to fill a niche. There was real fear that knitting was a dying craft, and I remember brainstorming sessions on how to attract young knitters. Back then, as now, knitters were happy to share our skills, but the prospect of participating in an "old ladies'" activity held little appeal.

At long last, in the late 1990s, the stars formed a constellation that drew in new and lapsed knitters as the knitting lives of Julia Roberts, Mary-Louise Parker, Daryl Hannah, Cameron Diaz, and other celebrities were featured with increasing regularity in the media. And thus a multigenerational support group was already in place in the wake of September 11, 2001, as women shared knowledge, time, problems, solutions, ideas, stories, laughter, and tears.

Knitting reemerged as a powerful connection when we needed it the most. It is as if a healing wisdom finally sprang out through our DNA. It became acceptable to knit in public, at bars, in coffeehouses, and at other gathering places. The craft many of us learned at grandma's knee became a "cool" connector.

In 2003 Debbie Stoller wrote in *Stitch 'n' Bitch: The Knitter's Handbook*, "It was exactly the gendered nature of the craft that drew me to it.... Betty Friedan and other like-minded feminists had overlooked an important aspect of knitting when they viewed it simply as part of women's societal obligation to serve everyone around them—they had forgotten that knitting served the knitter as well."[2]

In her 1981 book, *Addiction to Perfection,* Marion Woodman lamented that a society that dishonors primal feminine instincts produces generations of mothers who do not own their femininity, so they "could not pass on their joy in living, their faith in being, their trust in life as it is [to their sons and daughters] ... nor can society offer a Great Mother image [for a daughter] to reach out to ... to bridge the gap between herself and her femininity. That archetype is not yet constellated."[3]

In the beginning of the twenty-first century, it appears from all accounts that knitting has emerged as a powerful female symbol that can put us back in touch with the harmony of life. The rich mythology, realities, and possibilities of knitting have brought us together to reexperience and reinvent its ways for ourselves, and to deepen the richness of the communal knowing. In its depths we can find a space to untangle the complications that keep us from finding and trusting who and what we really are—and ponder how we fit into the scheme of things.

In preparing to write this book, I've been engaged in a spiritual "untangling" with my friend Janice MacDaniels, which continues to be one of the most important growth experiences of my life. I met Janice when she worked at Patternworks, eventually comanaging the store. As a person who "folded her life in God's hands," Janice believed she did not get her job in Yarn Paradise by chance. Janice found the time for soul-satisfying knitting, which she first learned as a young mother from watching Elizabeth Zimmermann on TV, and went on to produce a series of "Unpatterns" to help other knitters find their wings. At Patternworks, I always valued her clear-thinking approach and often sought her counsel.

The surging popularity of knitting hit Patternworks like a great wave. We were suddenly out of room, time, and energy. Marvin and I realized that, at this stage in our lives, we needed to find someone else to ride the wave with Patternworks.

One day, when we were in the final stages of selling Patternworks, I was approached by Maura Shaw, an editor at SkyLight Paths (and mother of Nick Tantillo, the creator of the Project Wizard program used on the Patternworks website at the time), to write a book on knitting as a spiritual practice. At first, as a hardly observant Jew with no insight into spiritual issues (other than a vague belief in the mysteries of life), I didn't feel qualified for the project. But the timing synchronized perfectly with my freedom, and I was drawn to a spiritual exploration.

After almost a year of researching, living, and knitting, my original chapter ideas no longer rang true for me. In my struggle, I enlisted Janice to do a chapter on prayer shawls, thinking of her shawl "Unpattern" wisdom and active church involvement. After a few meetings, we found an energizing synergy in our explorations and so our separate journeys converged and a new path was begun. Its course brought us, and *The Knitting Way,* to places and people we would not have found alone: most important at the present moment, right into your hands.

1 Knitting into Awareness

Escape versus Care for the Soul

Knitting

Knitting defies a
Mass-produced culture that shuns
subsistence, handmade clothes,
clothes which will be kept forever.
This sort of activity does not
improve the GNP.

I once dreaded
knots. Gordian knots,
greyish knots in
rain-soaked shoelaces,
sour knots in my
nervous stomach.
Knitting creates beauty
from knots.

Knitting is old women with
blue-veined Aran patterns on the
backs of their pale hands. As they work
together, they discuss food, children,
crops, politics, sweet passions, and
cold husbands.

I teach
Lisa how to knit.

She struggles,
drops stitches, her
cat eats the yarn.
We are not cosmopolitan
right now; we are our
grandmothers, we are artisans, we are
revolutionaries.

Knitting is meditation. The
steady click of the needles is a
rosary, a mantra, chanting monks.
This unprofitable chore is therapy
worth $60 an hour. I can not afford
not to knit.

I knit a
cardigan for Dani.
Energy flows down my
arms and hands, through
fingertips and shiny
needles, into each unique stitch of this
sweater that will
hug her warm in January.

—Cris Carusi[1]

Fate and knitting crossed all of our paths and brought us here, to be together. Once upon a time, in places far away, we began our separate journeys and, so, we all have much to tell about how we started, how it is now, and how we got here. It was the joining of separate stories that brought *The Knitting Way* into being and how it evolved. There's so much to help all of us on the path. The spiritual depth in knitting is without end. Together we'll explore some of its openings to new ways of seeing that lead us on a journey of discovery. Let's enter our story, right now, through the opening of Janice's "Space between the Loops."

Space between the Loops

The River of Connection

Listen to the music of knitting. The knitting melody flows, carrying each one of us along a river of connection. Find the kind of music it is for you. It doesn't really matter what kind of music. Just let it speak to you and open your soul to wonders.

Hear the wind, the sea, and the rolling hills. Listen to the sky. Let your hands dance with the wool. Your fingers see the sheep on the green hills. The smell of the earth that produced the grass that fed the sheep who gave their fleece lies in the wool. The sound is in the wool. Hear the waves, the sea air, the salt spray that nurtured the wild sheep in the Shetlands and Hebrides. The harmony is found there. It calls us to remember and reach for the comfort of the work of our hands.

Knitting's music reflects lovers, children, mothers and fathers, friends—good and bad. The knitting song transports us to other places, other times. This fiber symphony crosses cultures and takes us to faraway places. It ties us to traditions that may not be our own, yet we feel kinship.

Knitting connects us to all who have gone before. It links us to the past, to those who knitted for their existence, who knitted for survival, who knitted for beauty and love. It links us to our own past. We can know our ancestors who knitted. We can experience their past in our fingers. A knitting great-grandmother is still in our fingers. The orchestra connects us, not just by blood and DNA but by the stitch.

A grand concert of beauty, history, earth, and sky lies in the work of our hands. Knitting has melody, harmony, and rhythm. Hear it. It is music. Listen.

> *Music hath charms to soothe the savage breast,*
>   *To soften rocks, or bend a knotted oak.*

—William Congreve, *The Mourning Bride*

Looking for the Way

I began my retirement from Patternworks in an expectant state of mind. Old pressures were winding down and a new opportunity to write this book was before me. But I didn't have a clue about the spiritual path of knitting, which is apparent in this piece I wrote at a writing workshop at the local library.

> I just retired. This is the first partial free day after selling my business. Jeff, the sign man, came to take down the letters and signs that he put up six years ago when we moved into the new building. Everyone's been wishing Marvin and me luck. They say we deserve it. Perhaps I'm too young for retirement. I think of it as the time I need to explore the world and myself in new ways. This workshop came at an auspicious time. One of my plans is to write, specifically on how to become saner or more effective. And, that it's never too late, with me as an example.
>
> I saw the business as a vehicle for my creativity until I noticed that I was aging in dog years and my health was being compromised. Actually, the first sign came when we moved to the new building. I applied for life insurance to cover the five-year lease and my required checkup put me in a higher-rate category.

So, with this limited mindset, I embarked on a search for the River of Connection, entering it from where I was, the only place I could start. Janice had long ago encountered territory on the spiritual path that I was yet to discover. But this is a journey, I learned, not bound by time and place. As Janice explained to me, "What comes out of 'your doing' you must accept. When you don't let what comes, come, you can get into a rut and you'll miss an unexpected journey." Our common vehicle was yarn and knitting needles, so astride our knitting into the tangles and ruts we cast on, each on our own journey, but together in spirit. I had a spiritual friend!

Daily life in Yarn Paradise.

Our weekly meetings are a cross between a playgroup, a prayer meeting, an encounter session, a show-and-tell, and a birthing. We drink tea and explore. We search for clues. The hours go by and our minds expand. Curiously, we don't often knit together. Why? Yes, why? Maybe we don't need to knit together. Maybe it's enough for the two of us to explore the state of knit verbally, through our hearts, minds, and eyes. The knitting is still there, a presence that waits when we are together, to come back to our hands when we are apart.

Where am I right now? In trying to tell my story about the Knitting Way, I still get caught in old tangles. But the essence of what I've encountered along the path came to me in the middle of the night. I typed: "Spaciousness! I snapped awake. A new dimension sprang out ... an answer that put all this together. When I got to the keyboard, it had gone. Inaccessible. Frustration. Was it a dream?"

Spaciousness—I think that's it! Reading Janice's musings and the wisdom of other travelers in the "Space between the Loops" refreshes a memory of spaciousness somewhere down deep. Tuning into the rhythms within and around me, "listening for the music," is a new part of my story. I feel like I'm learning to be a musician and a dancer, to join in the performance of life, when before I didn't notice there was music or a dance. My own clutter hid what was right there, on the Knitting Way.

I had many hints along the way, such as this one from writer Brenda Ueland in *Strength to Your Sword Arm.* "In order to listen, here are some suggestions: Try to learn tranquility, to live in the present a part of the time every day. Sometimes say to yourself: 'Now. What is happening now? This friend is talking. I am quiet. There is endless time. I hear it, every word.' Then suddenly you begin to hear not only what people are saying, but also what they are trying to say, and you sense the whole truth about them. And you sense existence, not piecemeal, not this object and that, but as a translucent whole."[2]

But there's nothing harder or easier. Old habits die hard. I've found out firsthand the truth that "learning to listen is a spiritual art form that takes practice," as Sherry Anderson and Patricia Hopkins wrote in *The Feminine Face of God.* Knitting brings soul mates to practice with.

Are you reading this book because you share our enthusiasm for knitting? That's how Janice and I wound up on a path together. There's nothing we'd like better than if you'd join us. Microbiologist René Dubos, in his masterpiece *A God Within*, called *enthusiasm* "the most beautiful word in any language ... meaning far more than deep interest, ardent zeal, or twinkling eyes." *Enthusiasm* is from the Greek *entheos*, which means "a god within" and is the source of all creativity. That's why our knitting can be an opening to all that is.

"The opposite of the holy is the superficial," according to Marc Gafni in *Soul Prints.* So to honor the craft of knitting is to encounter the Holy. Stopping at the superficial is getting caught in the trap of limiting ourselves to what can be seen or measured; in other words, the trap of materialism.

The problems with materialism are clearly laid out by Maurice Nicoll in *Living Time and the Integration of the Life.* Trying to get our sense of existence from external things means that we are trying to *feel* ourselves in something outside ourselves. Impossible! Talk about looking in all the wrong places. We feel that what we lack lies *out there*. It's natural to view the world this way, Nicoll says, because the "world of sense is obvious." We think the solution to our problems is getting something or getting recognition. While the obvious world, perceived through our senses, fascinates us, we don't reflect that we may be "related to another world ... through 'understanding.'... Our inner life—*oneself*—has no position in that space which is perceptible to the senses."

This sounds like another paradox, but only on the surface. That's what I'm discovering. Everything's different beyond the surface. Beyond the dead outer skin is where the juice of life exists. Listening to the music begins with listening to your "inner life"—the realm of the soul. "Care of the soul requires a special crafting of life itself, with an artist's sensitivity to the way things are done.... Care of the soul begins with observance of how the soul manifests itself and how it operates. We can't care for the soul unless we are familiar with its ways," writes Thomas Moore in *Care of the Soul.*

Moore goes on to say, "Observance is a word from ritual and religion. It means to watch out for, but also to keep and honor, as in the observance of a holiday. The *-serv-* in *observance* originally referred to tending sheep. Observing the soul, we keep an eye on its sheep, on whatever is wandering and grazing—the latest addiction, a striking dream, or a troubling mood.... Observance of the soul can be deceptively simple. You take back what has been disowned."[3] The Knitting Way is a path to bring observance into our daily spiritual lives.

"In many ways our mass-produced household items of today, clothes, tools and utensils, look so much slicker and more professional than items from the past, that we can be misled into thinking that everything used to be cruder and more roughly made, but if we consider the creative process involved in hand crafts, this is absolutely not the case ... and if we look at knitted pieces carried out as recently as fifty years ago in a less hurried world, the work was often very much finer and more intricate than we would consider making today," said British knitter Alison Ellen in her inspiring book for the adventurous knitter, *Hand Knitting: New Directions,* published in 2002.[4] The trend is changing, as knitters become immersed in a culture that honors the craft of life.

To see beneath the surface takes some solitude every day. Fortunately, our knitting can come along, but only if we vow that we won't keep the practice from our inner-most self, because that's what the time is for. Capturing the time every day for an intimate encounter of this kind is part of the adventure.

Paradoxically, modern conveniences ostensibly give us more leisure time but actually take from us the time we need to attend to the art of living. For example, an article in the *New York Times* in 2004 about cell phone use in national parks, the places and spaces in which we tradi-tionally communed with nature, said that some conserva-tionists blamed cell phone technology not only for ruining nature "by scarring the landscape with cell towers but also by contributing to the death of solitude." And, ominously, in the same newspaper there was an article titled "After the Double Helix: Unraveling the Mysteries of the State of Being," which quoted Dr. Francis Crick, one of the codis-coverers of DNA, as saying he was working on "neural correlates of consciousness" that "will lead to the death of

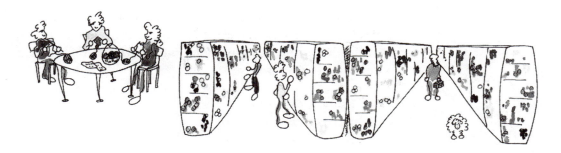

the soul." Dr. Crick died several months later, presumably leaving his work unfinished.

In the face of these challenges, there's no time like the present to begin unraveling our own mysteries of being. "The meaning of our existence is not invented by ourselves, but rather detected," observed Victor Frankl, a psychoanalyst who was a concentration camp survivor. We can find clues we need on the Knitting Way.

It always amazed me at Patternworks, which wasn't called Yarn Paradise for nothing, to see some first-time knitters sail through the selection of the pattern and yarn for a project and knit exactly the garment they had in mind, while others (a group that has included me) agonized with less inspired results.

I particularly remember one young woman who had just learned to knit from some friends who had convened a small knitting group. She came in alone to select her first project and picked a simple sweater from *Vogue Knitting* in a yarn and color that pleased her. I have to admit that when she wore in the finished sweater, which looked fabulous on her, I felt jealous. There I was with probably hundreds of techniques in my hands and the same choices available, yet my current projects did not work as well for me as that one did for her.

Janice attributes it to "vision." You need a vision of where you want to end up: what you're willing or able to deal with. Why make yourself crazy? As with life, there are too many variables to be able to be in complete control, so your vision needs to be dynamic, adjusting to conditions. Do the best you can and accept the rest. As far as getting help, you have to:

1. Know you need it.
2. Know how to ask for it.
3. Be willing to take it.
4. Ask the right people.
5. Be able to guide your helpers to get to what you need.
6. Actively listen to what they tell you.
7. Make an informed decision.

Do you see how this applies to more than the knitting?

In the store the potential selector (including the owner) could be overwhelmed by the possible choices, although I remember one woman who walked in and said, "You don't have anything!"—an example of how we create the world we live in. I needed to address my personal "issues" in order to come away feeling satisfied. We'll go deeper into how our personal issues affect our projects in chapter 8, "Bearing Witness."

Knitting has a lot to tell us about how we're navigating in the world. It's also a guide in expanding our horizons.

What We Think We See

This may come as a shock to anyone who's been to a yarn shop or attended that festive explosion of yarn, color, knitters, and vendors called "Stitches Market," but neurologist Sir John Elles tells us, "I want you to realize that there exists no color in the natural world, and no sound—nothing of this kind; no textures, no patterns, no beauty, no scent." It's hard to believe, but everything we see is a construct of the mind.

Science—which as you may know seems to be on its own spiritual journey, going deeper and deeper beyond appearances and finding connections everywhere—tells us we live in a sea of electromagnetic energy that's transmitted in three-dimensional waves from the sun.

Light is the only part of the electromagnetic spectrum that is visible to us, coming between the longer waves—radio, microwave, infrared (which we experience as heat)—and the progressively shorter ultraviolet rays (which burn our skin), x-rays, and gamma rays. A light wave can be reflected, absorbed, or transmitted, depending on the object the wave hits, and that will give it its color. For a ball of yarn to look black, all the wavelengths of light hitting it are absorbed; no light is reflected. Solid objects, for the most part, will reflect light, and transparent objects will transmit light through them.

When light falls on the retina of the eye, tiny, distorted, upside-down images are produced and fed to the brain. This is a *sensation*. Sensation takes place when the sensory organs passively (without our conscious involvement) bring information from the outside into the body and send coded electrical impulses to the brain through the neurons. The brain decodes these impulses into an image that "makes sense" in a process called *perception*. The brain, which has been preprogrammed in a stock set of responses through the genes and experiences, automatically makes the easiest, most obvious connection in order to efficiently handle the incessant barrage of input. It says, for instance, "tree."

Here's where awareness comes in. We need to be actively involved to get beyond this biased, limited, and limiting, surface report—to be there and aware in knitting and in life. In the Renaissance, Leonardo da Vinci told us what he saw beyond the surface. "Here, right here in the eye, here forms, here colors, right here the character of every part and everything of the universe, are concentrated to a single point.... In this small space the universe can be completely reproduced and rearranged in its entire vastness!" Da Vinci revealed how imagination opened the world he lived in. "Imagination was the most important failure" leading to the September 11 attacks, concluded the bipartisan 9/11 Commission in the summer of 2004. Modern conveniences demand little imagination. Fortunately, our knitting does. Without imagination we're stuck in a box of our own making. Through our knitting story we can, like da Vinci, open the universe within ourselves.

Space between the Loops
What Do You See?

The act of knitting can be an influential activity for all parts of life. It can slow us to rest. It can offer us its hand of companionship, give us warmth, and teach us trust. It can also be used as a training ground to help us look at the tiny, inside-out parts of our lives. Seeing what really *is,* is far different from seeing what we think we see. Our eyes see a tree, but our brains, maybe because we are impatient, say, "Yes, yes a tree. Up and down, brown trunk and some green stuff on top, move on." We have failed to really see the tree.

The science of seeing gets more interesting. Two types of images exist in nature: real and virtual. In a real image, the light rays actually come from the image. In a virtual image, they only appear to come from a reflected image. For example, the virtual image of your face appears to be "inside" the mirror because the pattern of light reflected from your face is reflected back by the mirror.

But real images can also form in a region of space away from the object, if emerging light rays, from both the object and a "reference" beam, cross to form a new light pattern. This pattern is called "interference" because the intersecting light wave patterns affect one another. The reference beam is a portion of the same light that was intercepted and directed to a particular region of space *before* it got to the object. The part of the light that strikes and reflects off the object is directed to the same place as the reference beam, and so they intersect and form an interference pattern.

That's how holograms are created. Holograms are exact recordings, on light-sensitive holographic film, of the light waves reflected from an object at its intersection with a reference beam. This process captures, or encodes, every nuance of the interference-pattern event in time and space. We experience an exact replica of the event when the reference beam is reintroduced.

Unlike a photograph taken with a camera that presents an image from a single, unchangeable, two-dimensional viewpoint, holograms record all the visual information of the scene, including depth, actually making space visible! It allows us to view the scene from many angles because every part of the hologram contains the message of the entire image as seen from its particular angle. Several events can be recorded on top of each other to capture these events as they take place in time.

Isn't knitting like a hologram? Like our signatures, each stitch is a unique expression of the way we are at that moment—of our mental and physical state, where we've been and where we're going. The sweater is a record of our lives at particular moments in time. Janice and I discussed this in our weekly meeting, after I brought up the way Betty Smith captures a moment in time in *A Tree Grows in Brooklyn,* the book-on-tape I was listening to in the car. In my new spiritually aware state, I seemed to hear wisdom on every recorded "page."

It was April 6, 1917, and Francie Nolan, our heroine, found a newspaper hot off the press on her desk with the six-inch headline "WAR." "Francie had a vision. Fifty years from now, she'd be telling her grandchildren how she had come to the office, sat at her reader's desk and in the routine of work had read that war had been declared. She knew from listening to her grandmother that old age was made up of such remembrances of youth. But she didn't want to recall things. She wanted to live things—or as a compromise relive rather than reminisce."[5]

Francie understood that it was necessary to notice and absorb every sight, sound, touch, and smell in this space in order to suspend it in time. She reverently prepared a time capsule, including the front page of the newspaper, her inky fingerprints impressed on a white piece of paper and underlined with her lipstick, a new 1917 penny, and a worn clipping of a poem by a "Brooklyn poet" that she reread twenty times before sealing it all in an envelope. On the outside she signed: "Frances Nolan, age 15 years and 4 months. April 6, 1917." Our knitting projects are our time capsules.

The poem that held so much meaning for Francie is by Walt Whitman.

> I am of old and young, of the foolish as much as the
>   wise;
> Regardless of others, ever regardful of others.
> Maternal as well as paternal, a child as well as a
>   man,
> Stuff'd with the stuff that is coarse, and stuff'd with
>   the stuff that is fine.

Janice told her own story of a knitted time capsule.

Space between the Loops
Memories from the Vest

I take the vest out of the storage box that I keep under my bed and I am transported. We had loaded the station wagon and made our way to the Adirondack Mountains for our annual fishing vacation. This last week in August assured us that the campground would be relatively empty and, as usual, we had the run of the place.

It was the last week to say goodbye to Lady Summer and get ready to greet the cooling skies of September, the routines of school and pumpkin days of fall. We spent warm, idyllic days fishing from the floating dock or the shiny aluminum boat, its oars like wings over the water. We took lazy afternoon swims at the empty beach surrounded by the strong arms of the mountains, the silver sunlight coins dancing on the lake. Late night sunsets graced us, bathed us in lavender beauty as we gathered around the ancient campfire, splendidly and competitively ignited by the family pyromaniacs.

With the diamond blanket of God's Milky Way covering us, the nights were filled with stories of the big one that got away, verses of "Home, Home on the Range," "Clementine," and blazing marshmallows trailing their flame path in the darkness. When the fire was extinguished, the steam from the dying embers still hissing, we retired to the kitchen table inside the hodge-podge cabin. Sitting in the mismatched chairs, our late-night poker games were fierce and played with the intensity of any high-stakes game in Las Vegas, all for the winnings of burnt matches. Vacation nights run late, but bedtime does come, reluctantly. Snuggling down into the well-worn and always-springy beds for sleep, the nights were cold enough for the woodstove and the cold on our noses lasted all night because the wood did not.

Memories are relived as the vest is brought out of the cedar chest.[6]

I brought knitting to do. This year I brought the yarn and needles for the vest that lay before me, a cream-color homespun yarn full of lanolin and yummy. From start to finish I knitted the vest during one week of our vacation in the Adirondacks. Funny how seeing it, touching it, brings back the time and place. This vest holds the Adirondack Mountains, the lake, and my young children for me. It's all there in my mind's eye and memory. My knitting holds the whole of the memories of my life, the times, the people and places for when I need to visit them again.

19

We Plan and God Laughs

It surprised me to find out that the supposedly upright (and uptight) square and its three-dimensional expansion, the cube, are not as stable as we stack them up to be. Don't most of us live in cubes? Actually, squares and cubes are contrived, human creations, not found in nature. Janice had a vivid demonstration of nature's power when she felted the toy block she had knitted for her grandchild. Read her true story in the form of a fairy tale: "The Cube That Wanted to Be a Ball."

Space between the Loops
The Cube That Wanted to Be a Ball

Once there was a grandma who lived near the woods in an old brown and white farmhouse and she was given the gift of a grandson. She loved to knit, and knowing that little ones love soft and cozy playthings she set about to make a marvelous toy for the child. She searched for the perfect object and came upon the idea for a knitted block, a cube. There would be six little sides to shine all the love and kisses of a grandma. She carefully thought about the colors to use and after settling upon three, her needles clicked away and the wooly yarn danced through her fingers.

She knitted the first side and said, "This side is for the green of summers ahead when the lazy clouds and butterflies float by." She knitted the second side and said, "This side is for the rose of sunsets and flowers on the pathway." The third side was knitted and the grandma said, "This side is for Christmas green and birthday surprises to come." The fourth side spoke up and said, "I am for pink strawberries and candy-times at Grandma's house." The fifth and six sides were each white, and after a time, the grandma said that they were for the pureness of babies and winter snow.

The knitting was done and the grandma decided that a baby toy should be jingle-y and went to her Striped Katie

Cat to ask for permission to use one of her jingle bell balls. Katie Cat meowed. Grandma knew that meant, "Yes." She placed the jingle bell ball inside the cube, stuffed it up tight with fluffy stuffing, and using a sharp sewing needle, worked all of the seams.

It was a beautiful cube, a block for the new baby boy, but the grandma wanted to make the fabric all tight and firm so the cube would sit square upon the floor. She went to her washtub and washboard. She filled it with hot water and sudsy bubbles and the grandma scrubbed the little cube until it shrank and tightened up. It became fuzzy and felted, but the cube seemed different. Something was at work. She placed the cube on a table to dry and went to bed. In the morning, the grandma hurried down her stairs to check on the cube and discovered that it was no longer a cube but had changed into a ball.

"How can this be?" she wondered. "What did I do wrong?" She had used the proper yarn, the proper needles, and the proper pattern. She had made all the proper stitches. She had knitted, stuffed and sewn, and washed and felted properly. Everything had been done right, yet there was a ball instead of a cube.

The grandma didn't understand but the day came when the baby boy came to visit. He was just learning to balance himself and sit up on a blanket on the floor. The grandma gave the baby the new toy, with apologies to the mother for it being a ball and not a cube. Then a wonderful thing happened. The grandson grabbed the ball in his chubby hand, hearing the jingle, squealed a baby giggle, and gave it a toss. What joy! It rolled, and the colors were spinning and dancing all around. The ball played so smartly with the grandson, rolling about and jingling. It was just one of many happy afternoons at grandma's house. The grandma knew right then that a soft ball was the proper toy for a grandson and the heart of the cube knew it, too. She was glad that the cube knew better.

Nature centers into balls,
And her proud ephemerals,
Fast to surface and outside,
Scan the profile of the sphere;
Knew they what that signified,
A new genesis were here.

—Ralph Waldo Emerson, *Circles: An Essay*

Experience It for Yourself

Learning to let things be what they are, to trust, comes hard to some of us. Think about the times when it is hard for you to have faith that things will work out in your own life as you create your own ball from a cube.

Ball from a Cube

Felting is a risky business. Placing wool in hot water and agitating it goes against our natural understanding of what you are supposed to do to wool. This requires a bit of trust. Use worsted weight yarn, 100% wool, and size US 9 or 10 needles. Choose up to 6 colors (one for each "side"). I used a 100% wool batting/stuffing to stuff this toy. You will also need a new jingle bell cat toy. The stitch pattern is garter stitch.

Using 2 strands worked together and color A, cast on 20 stitches and knit 40 rows (20 ridges). Change to color B and continue for 40 more rows (20 ridges).

Do the same for colors C and D. You now have a strip of 4 different color squares.

On each side of the *color B square,* using E and F respectively, pick up 20 stitches (one at each ridge) and knit 40 rows. You now have a piece that looks a bit like a cross, composed of 6 squares.

Following the diagram on page 23, fold the *A, E, and F squares* up so that their sides meet.

Before.

After.

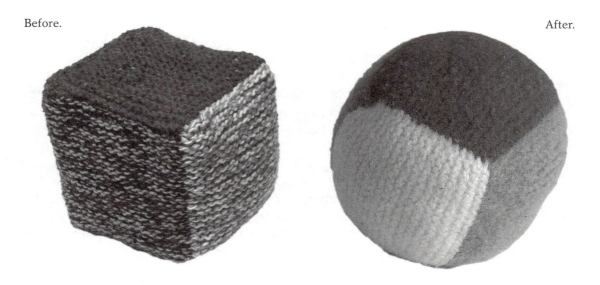

The Cube That Wanted to Be a Ball: Nature and knitting have their way.

Sew together at those edges.

Fold at the C–B intersection and sew to the adjacent sides of E and F.

D becomes the little top. Sew it to E and F.

Leave the side next to A open and stuff, inserting an unused jingle bell cat toy.

Sew D to A.

Felting: Using the hottest water, the lowest amount of water, and the highest agitation your washing machine can provide, place piece in machine with small amount of laundry soap and agitate for 10–15 minutes. Check piece to see if the fibers are shrinking and locking. If needed, continue

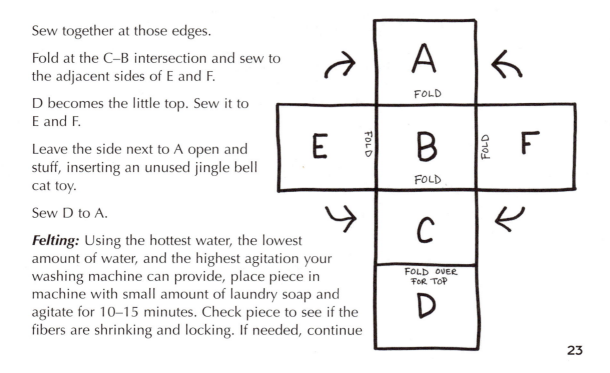

this agitation process, in 10-minute increments, until you are satisfied with the results. Remove from machine and rinse thoroughly at the sink with cold water (which causes the fibers to "seize" even more). Drain in a colander and squeeze out excess water in a towel. Re-shape and allow to dry thoroughly. Hopefully, you now have a ball instead of a cube! If not, trust the wool. It is what it is supposed to be.

Chizu Nakamura, a Japanese knitter who was part of the Fushiginoiroito workshop described in chapter 4, "Once Upon a Time: The Stories of Our Projects," told of her own experience with wool. "I am an ordinary woman from a country that has used wool for a relatively short period.... Although wool first came to Japan in the sixteenth century, it wasn't until the twentieth that ordinary people started to use it. It seems to be my duty to pass a message to the assembled ranks of fellow enthusiasts, with your long and honorable tradition of using wool. My message: 'I recently discovered that wool, in addition to all its other useful qualities, has a healing power when you touch it.'" Many of us have noticed that there's something especially comforting about knitting with wool.

Science, Mystery, and Knitting
A New Way of Looking at Things

A Knitter's Understanding of Very Basic, but Mysterious, Modern Physics

Henry Miller said, "One's destination is never a place but rather a new way of looking at things." And as Janice pointed out, faith, a basic foundation of spirituality, is defined in the book of Hebrews (11:1) as "the substance of things hoped for, the evidence of things not seen," meaning that trust, itself, is the evidence. Faith is a way of looking at things that yields to "the pull toward beauty, intelligibility, truth, value, and company without restriction.... transcendentals that have no intrinsic limitations—we can always seek more," according to Tad Dunne in the article "Spiritual Care at the End of Life" in *Hastings Center Magazine.* Having faith and trust in our knitting as we go along the Knitting Way means giving up the myth that we have total control in order to let our knitting open us to new possibilities that we didn't see before. I've learned to revel in what happens when I'm knitting—often something quite different than what I had planned, as you'll see as we go along. Faith in the mystery of life is a big part of the Knitting Way. At the start of my journey, I found that the new sciences bolstered my faith, since they show that our world *is* essentially rooted in mystery—and we probably will never be able to completely understand it through scientific methods alone. Science certainly helped me look at things (not just my knitting) in a new way. I thought you might like to take a look with me.

Einstein showed that matter and energy—which make up everything in the universe—are two forms of the same thing. Everything physical—our hands, the air, yarn, our tea, and this book—is called matter, composed of atoms surrounded by nearly mass-less electrons that have a negative charge (in the traditional solids, liquids, and gases, that is).

Electromagnetic force keeps the negatively charged particles of your hands from making actual contact with the particles that make up this book. No matter how hard you squeeze, you can't make them touch. All that's in contact is the force between the electrons. Stand up, and it's the thin layer of electromagnetic force that supports you. Your body doesn't actually touch the floor! This concept gives new meaning to being "light on your feet," and it's something to ponder as you handle your luscious yarns.

Things start getting even more interesting in the fourth state of matter, called plasma, which is composed of free-floating electrons and ions (positively charged atoms that have had their electrons ripped away). Plasma (different from biological plasma) accounts for 99 percent of the known mass of the universe. The sun emits streams of plasma that create solar winds. These interact with the earth's magnetic field, causing a geomagnetic "tail" on our night side and aurora light shows at the north and south poles. Lightning is an example of plasma on earth, and plasmas are used in neon and fluorescent lights, computer chips, and plasma TV screens. Plasma fusion is a powerful potential source of energy for the future.

Recently, scientists have been creating new forms of matter in labs. The fifth form is a superfluid, the Bose-Einstein condensate, made up of tightly bound particles (first produced in 1995) that "are not vaporous, not hard, not fluid.... Indeed, there are no ordinary words to describe them because they come from another world— the world of quantum mechanics," says an article on the NASA website, titled "A New Form of Matter." Quantum mechanics is a study of the smallest particles and their interactions.

The sixth form of matter, a fermionic condensate that was created in 2004, is another superfluid related to a Bose-Einstein condensate, but more difficult to produce. It could lead to new ways of transmitting electricity. Our world is getting bigger all the time.

Some Deep Mysteries That Still Loom

Physicists at the end of the nineteenth century thought we were close to having all the answers about what makes the universe tick. Now at the beginning of the twenty-first century it's becoming ever clearer how little we actually understand. A map of the universe taken by satellite gives the following picture of matter and energy in our world: Atoms (which we're still learning about) account for 4 percent; dark matter (which we have guesses about) accounts for 24 percent; and dark energy (about which we have no clue) accounts for 72 percent. Cosmologists admit that they're baffled by the role of life in the cosmos. Science has given us a lesson in how pride, which we're warned against in all the wisdom traditions, can blind the eye.

Although modern physics leaves us with more questions than answers, it does give us evidence of the River of Connection. Science writer Dennis Overbye sums up: "Physicists are telling us particle physics has not been about particles for a long time.... Rather it is about the relationships between particles, the symmetries that nature seems to respect ... the beauty that physical laws seem to embody.... Physicists think they have a pretty good story to tell these days.... But the real best seller here is wonder."

Let's see—scientific experiments have already demonstrated:

- The answer to whether light is a wave or a particle is "yes."
- When we try to measure the location of a particle we disturb it in some way.

- Electrons can spontaneously appear and disappear on different sides of a barrier at speeds faster than light, disturbing the classic rules of cause and effect. (This is called quantum tunneling. Subatomic particles can apparently exist in two places at the same time, making no distinction between time and space.)
- Every quantum particle in the universe has a mirror image of itself that's called antimatter. (Positrons are the positively charged antimatter counterpart of electrons.)
- When particles of matter collide with particles of antimatter, they annihilate one another, providing one of the most powerful sources of energy in the universe.
- Two particles can become "entangled" so that even when separated by huge distances, a change in one particle will cause a spontaneous change in the other (another case of communication faster than the speed of light).
- In this "dance" an atom can spin both clockwise and counterclockwise at the same time! (This is called the Einstein-Podolsky-Rosen effect, or quantum connectedness.)

On the quantum subatomic level, space, which we used to think of as an empty vacuum, is filled with fluctuating energy. (This is called zero-point energy, which could be more powerful than matter/antimatter reactions.) Zero-point energy produces virtual particles, called *virtual* because they so quickly form antimatter and disappear back into the vacuum. "Quantum mechanics presents logically opposing situations, mutually exclusive states, and then insists that they coexist.... The theory nonetheless makes extremely accurate predictions and hasn't failed any tests.... Reality, in at least some aspects, seems to depend on the observer," summarizes cosmologist Janna Levin in *How the Universe Got Its Spots,* and then she adds, "I don't know the answers, but it does give us some divine questions to ask."[1] We can use our knitting as a vehicle that gives us the space we need to question the Divine as we reflect on the big questions of our lives. That's what we're doing on the Knitting Way.

Scientists are still looking for a Theory of Everything (TOE) that explains all the forces of the universe (it eluded Einstein). George Johnson, another science writer who makes these confusing concepts clear, presented this philosophical view of the possibility of scientists explaining everything in an article in the *New York Times*: "But then they would have to find a law to explain where the law came from ... and ultimately an explanation of why the universe is mathematical and of where mathematics came from and what numbers are. Like a petulant eight-year-old, we keep asking why, why, why, why. In the end, the answer is either 'just because' or 'for God made it so.' Take your pick."

I feel a knitting break coming on, and you probably do, too. All this science can make your head spin, but first, let's get to some of the "answers," and some questions to ponder as we knit.

The most widely accepted theory for explaining quantum phenomena says that a particle is what you measure it to be. When it looks like a particle, it *is* a particle. When it looks like a wave, it *is* a wave. In other words, *nothing is real unless it is observed*. Danish physicist Niels Bohr, the author of the theory, said, "We must be clear, that when it comes to atoms, language can be used only as in poetry." How can we ever understand? "I think we may yet be able to do so. But in the process we may have to learn what the word 'understanding' really means."

Another physicist, David Bohm, who worked closely with Einstein, developed the theory of active information, one of the multi-universe theories. It proposes that a universe exists for every potential outcome, but when a particular path is taken, the other universes are no longer accessible. In other words, if you mistake a tree for an attacker on a dark night, thus choosing a particular path, the *meaning* of the tree is changed, actually making electrochemical changes in your mind and body and causing a restructuring of nerve pathways and connections. Therefore, according to Bohm, "A change of meaning is a change of being."

Another attempt to explain quantum phenomena is superstring theory, which posits that instead of living in a three-dimensional world, we're actually enfolded in multi-dimensions. Janna Levin says, "We're oblivious to the extra dimensions because in a sense we're too big to notice that they're there." There are actually several superstring theories, and it's said that all of them may be true!

As Janice commented when we were talking about these theories, "The new complexities of science do show things weirder and weirder all the time. I remember a TV show on Einstein, and the man being interviewed said that scientists look at Einstein's equation and weep. Now, what do they see that we don't? Obviously something, if the beauty of that little, silent equation brings them to tears. That is spiritual. God's power and creative force are in those formulas, all over science, and every now and then, God presents us with a person, a mind, to which God has revealed the hidden. We are finite, and when we are presented with the increasingly infinite (because God is infinite), which scientists are continually discovering ... we say 'Wow, God!' Well, I do anyway."

Microbiologist René Dubos points out in a chapter he calls "On Being Human" in *The God Within* that both religion and science "constitute deep-rooted and ancient efforts to find richer experience and deeper meaning," helping us recognize human life as an "adventure of the spirit." And, then, in a chapter called "A Demon Within," he explores how the technologies born of science, which were created by humans to act as our servants, have taken over in ways not conducive to human health or happiness. (And this book was written in 1971.)

Dubos ponders how and when we've gone astray since the eighteenth century, when the word *civilization* was first used. To the philosophers of the Enlightenment, *civilization* had feminine connotations, "considered the highest expressions of mankind ... gentle ways of life, humane laws, limitations on war, a high level of purpose and conduct." Dubos says that, sometime between the Chicago World's Fairs of 1893 and 1933 the organizers acquired the "technology religion" spelled out in the 1933 Fair's guidebook: "Science discovers, genius invents, industry applies and *man adapts himself to, or is molded by,* new things.... Individuals, groups, entire races of men *fall into step* with ... science and industry."

Dubos goes on to say that, although George Mallory's famous answer to the questioner who asked why he climbed Mount Everest, "Because it is there," exhibited human grandeur at the time, "the Mount Everest philosophy" isn't applicable to human society: It is an expression of compulsive animal behavior, like a bear or a raccoon moving to a garbage can. "The animal cannot escape from this compulsive behavior and therefore is readily caught in a trap. But man has more power of discrimination and greater freedom in selecting his course of action."[2] We knitters do select our course of action and in knitting we have the freedom to express the inherent beauty of our souls. That is a powerful ability.

Cris Carusi, who wrote the poem that opens chapter 1, said in e-mail to me: "I think that knitting is one way to address, and even protest, many of the problems that plague our culture. My poem pretty much sums this up to some degree. Knitting deepens connections between generations, slaps our shallow consumer values in the face, and creates a meaningful gift that defies dollars and cents."

When we tap into what's in our souls on the Knitting Way, we begin to notice a difference in our lives, and how much we influence the people around us. "There's no need for any new ideology, but there is an urgent need for each of us to discover the truth of our existence—first-hand," recommends Steven Harrison in *Doing Nothing: Coming to the End of the Spiritual Search.* He goes on to say, "Whatever understanding we may come to in our lives, it is not solely for our benefit. Our discovery is meaningful only in relationship, of which communication is the expression. The word communication shares its roots with communion, an act of sharing, and community, which is a unified body of individuals.... There is a very simple discovery that we may make as we investigate the nature of our world. This discovery is that while it may appear that we are just in the world, in fact, we find that we are the world."[3] We all, individually and together in the community of knitters, have a subtle, but powerful influence on what happens in the world.

Take Comfort in the Shapes of Nature

Nature loves spirals, and so does knitting. When you knit in the round, you're actually knitting a spiral. Spiritual growth progresses in a kind of spiral, too, rather than a straight line. Marion Woodman describes the journey of the Knitting Way in *Addiction to Perfection*, although she wasn't referring to knitting: "I prefer the pleasure of the journey through a spiral. And I ask my reader to relax and enjoy the spiral too. If you miss something on the first round, don't worry. You may pick it up on the second or the third or the ninth. It doesn't matter. The important thing is that you are relaxed so that if the bell does ring you will hear it and allow it to resonate through all the rungs of your own spiral. The world of the feminine resonates. Timing is everything. If it doesn't ring, either it is the wrong spiral or the wrong time or there is no bell."[4]

Space between the Loops
The Knitting Way Spiral

In *The Wizard of Oz*, Dorothy finds herself hurled far from Kansas to Munchkin Land, and in need of a way back. She meets Glinda, the good witch, who presents her with the ruby slippers from the feet of the wicked witch of the East and advises Dorothy, who is anxious to return to Kansas, to seek the way from the Wizard of Oz in the Emerald City. Since Dorothy hasn't got a broomstick, she must walk. She asks Glinda, "But how do I start for the Emerald City?" Glinda replies, "It's always best to start at the beginning—and all you do is follow the Yellow Brick Road." In the 1939 MGM film, the scene pulls back to reveal a yellow brick path that begins as a spiral. So Dorothy's journey home begins.

There are a couple of ancient Christian traditions, still used today, based on pathways: the labyrinth and the prayer walk. The labyrinth takes us on a directed journey from the outside to a center place of inner experience of the presence of God, and then brings us back out to a point of outward thinking and action. A labyrinth is different from a maze in that it only has one way to go, and we do not have to choose the direction we turn. A prayer walk is a path of contemplation and prayer, generally placed in an outdoor setting, but not always, taking any form, structured or meandering. It has a beginning point, and a point of closure and release, and may be directed by people or placards as spiritual guides. These paths are tools, structures, and containers that can hold us on our way.

Whether we know it or not, we are all on a path. The Knitting Way Spiral reminded me so much of *The Wizard of Oz*'s yellow brick road that I almost wished I had knitted it in yellow instead of a warm, golden olive. But more important, Glinda's advice to start at the beginning rings true, in that no matter where you find yourself on the path, you are at the beginning. Starting where you are is your beginning. Imagine yourself at the inner point of the spiral and wind your way out or imagine that you are beginning at the outer point and wind your way in, only to find that you may turn and wind your way out again. This knitted spiral symbolizes the journey, reminding us that no matter how many times you travel this knitting path you will learn something new. Simply walking the path is the value of walking the path. Moving forward from your own beginning to your own release is the point. It is a way home.

Experience It for Yourself

This spiral is a reminder that we are on a journey. As your hands work this pattern and as you make use of it during your walk along the path, reflect upon where you are along the journey and be content with your progress.

The Knitting Way Spiral

Knitting Way Spiral: As you move forward from your own beginning, you find your way home.

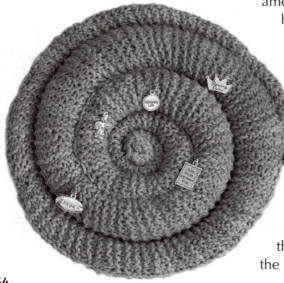

Use any worsted weight yarn and needles to give the gauge you like. I used a very textured cotton yarn with size US 3 needles and achieved a gauge of 4.5 stitches per inch. The amount of yarn will vary depending upon how large you wish your spiral to be. I used about 120 yards, polyfill or wool batting stuffing, and small charms or beads from the local craft store. I found the perfect charms of encouragement in the "make your own greeting cards" section.

It is worked in garter stitch.

Cast on 3 stitches, marking the center stitch and the right side (RS).

Knit 8 rows or 4 ridges, always knitting the marked stitch on the RS and purling the marked stitch on the wrong side (WS).

Looking at the RS, this will give one vertical stockinette stitch along the whole center length of the piece.

Next row: *Increase Row*, RS increase 1 stitch before and after the marked center stitch (5 stitches total). Work 1 WS row. One ridge made.

Now continue as established, and at every 9th ridge work the increase row until you have a total of 19 stitches. Work straight for about 36 inches (or as long as you like), maintaining the marked stitch as established. Begin decreasing.

Decrease row: Decrease 1 stitch each side of the marked stitch at every 9th ridge until 3 stitches remain.

Work 8 rows (4 ridges) and bind off.

Fold the piece lengthwise, with the RS out, along the center 1 stockinette stitch and sew the edge stitches along each side together to form a tube. Lightly stuff the tube as you sew it up. Beginning at either end, coil and sew the tube into a spiral, securing it along the sewn seam and the single stockinette V. Weave in the ends. Attach your charms and/or beads as markers as you progress along your knitting path. Linda and I see this as a small accent pillow to use as a reminder of your path along the Knitting Way.

Searching for Patterns

Mathematics, like knitting, is a language that holds beauty and meaning in its patterns. "Knitting is inherently mathematical," says mathematician Sarah-Marie Belcastro. "Mathematics is, at heart, a search for patterns and for a deep understanding of how and why they occur," according to Kathleen M. Shannon and Michael J. Bardzell in their online article "Searching for Patterns in Pascal's Triangle." But, the solution for turning the heel of a sock is considered "women's work," as compared with the solution for bending a pipe at a right angle in a way that avoids bunch at the inside and stretching at the outside—which is thought of as "real math," according to math educator Mary Harris, who challenges the stereotype associated with feminine activities. In her online article, "An Example of Traditional Women's Work as a Mathematics Resource," she writes, "Male teachers are so unfamiliar with the construction and even the shape and size of their own garments that they cannot at first perceive that all you need to make a sweater (apart from the technology and tools) is an understanding of ratio."

Janice remembers designing and making sweaters for two of her brothers. "Knitting the sweaters to their specs, I did all the math and engineered a sweater. My father, who worked at the Kennedy Space Center as an engineer, asked why I worked so hard at all the measuring and math. Why didn't I just use a pattern that was already written? I thought it strange that an engineer would ask that, especially one who spent a good many months 'dumpster diving' at carpet stores for scraps in order to collect a garage full of pieces to mathematically and artfully construct into a living room carpet. Dad's reaction didn't seem to fit with the way I was raised. Part of the magic of knitting for me was to take nothing but a string, two needles, and mathematical equations and create something … a vastly spiritual thing."

Thirty years ago mathematicians called Benoit Mandelbrot's new geometry based on fractal structures an attempt to represent the messiness of nature, "crazy, wild, ridiculous, insane," Mandelbrot recalled, in a newspaper article announcing that he had won the 2003 Japan Prize for outstanding achievement in the science and technology of complexity. Fractals are shapes and phenomena actually made up of similar shapes within shapes. They're found throughout nature, from coastlines, snowflakes, trees, rocks, jets of water, clouds, galaxies in the universe, and our bodies to the self-organizational patterns of large groups and systems like weather and the stock market.

Fractal theory points out that with complex shapes, like yarn, our ordinary concept of dimension changes depending on our point of view. For example, you see the ball of yarn as a three-dimensional object at a range as close as a few inches; then, from an inch away, it looks like a mess of one-dimensional strands; then, even closer, you again see the fibers as three-dimensional.

The theory of fractal structures has helped us tackle difficult problems, from how to determine the spread of acid rain and other pollutants to optimizing antennae. In the article on Mandelbrot, John Briggs, a professor at Western Connecticut State University, gave high praise: "Mandelbrot brings us back to the sense of the wonder of things, without giving up the logic." Science has validated the wisdom teaching that the whole world can be seen in a grain of sand—or in a stitch.

In 300 BCE, Euclid of Alexandria, the founder of geometry, gave us the first clear definition of a mysterious number that later became known as the Golden Ratio. The definition appears in his work *Elements*, a thirteen-volume colossus on geometry and number theory. A line can be divided at a certain point in which the proportions between *the larger segment and the shorter segment* and between *the whole line and the larger segment* are equal. The ratio between the larger segment and the shorter segment is known as the Golden Ratio. Precisely calculated, it is the never-ending, never-repeating number 1.6180339887 ... (and on and on). It is not a whole number such as 1, 2, or 3. It is not a rational number such as the fractions ¼, ⅓, ¾. It is an irrational number (not a whole number or a fraction) and carries properties that have fascinated mathematicians, scientists, artists, musicians, and even psychologists. It is a number of harmonious proportions, perhaps even aesthetic or beauteous proportions, and part of its mystery is that it appears where it is least expected—the arrangement of apple seeds, the placement of rose petals, and the structures of many shells of mollusks—and it can be found in art and music such as Salvador Dalí's painting of the *Sacrament of the Last Supper* and Béla Bartók's musical compositions.

After reading about nature's spirals, I was amazed to notice how flowers, shells, trees, and other organisms tend to grow in fractal patterns explained by Fibonacci numbers and the Golden Ratio. Leonardo of Pisa, who went by the name Fibonacci (which means "son of Bonaccio") and is called the "greatest mathematician of the Middle Ages," devised a sequence of numbers to solve the problem of how fast rabbits could breed under ideal circumstances. I first read about the Fibonacci sequence in Jacqueline Fee's *The Sweater Workshop,* where she cites it as a potential stripe sequence "arrived at by starting with 1 and then continually adding the two previous numbers. In short: 1, 1, 2, 3, 5, 8, 13, 21, 34, and so on, for as many rabbits as you'd care to knit."

The Golden Ratio, 1.61803 or phi (pronounced fee), has a fascinating property related to this. Let's say you draw a rectangle with sides the length of successive Fibonacci numbers, such as 8 x 13, which approach the Golden Ratio. Then, remove a square from one end. The dimensions of the remaining rectangle will have the same proportion as the bigger rectangle. The smaller rectangle that was produced is smaller than the parent rectangle by a factor of phi. This process can be repeated infinitely (if it were possible to draw infinitely smaller and smaller rectangles), creating a series of nested rectangles and forming the kinds of logarithmic spirals found in a nautilus shell, the horns of goats, the shape of spider webs, and the flight takeoff line of certain bat colonies. Nature loves these spirals; you can see them (going in both directions in a Fibonacci sequence) in the sunflower's seeds, the pinecone and pineapple's bracts, the cauliflower's florets, in seashells, hurricanes, giant spiral galaxies, and the flight of a falcon. "Is God a mathematician?" asked Sir James Hopwood Jeans, the early twentieth-century English physicist who first proposed that matter is created continuously in the universe.

I tried to understand the Golden Ratio spiral by knitting it. As I played with the shaping, my first attempt got too wide too soon, but it made me envision an elegant collar. What emerged in my next attempt, however, was a skullcap. A rounded shape like a nautilus shell formed itself in my unsuspecting hands; this hugs the shape of the head in a pleasing, organic way. The Jewish custom of wearing a skullcap is not found in the Bible, but it is said to have been transferred to ordinary people from the high priest in the days of the Pharisees as a means of expressing awareness of, and respect for, God throughout the day. Today, many Jewish women wear skullcaps along with the men when they pray. Wearing a skullcap can be a reminder of your connection with the holy. You don't have to be Jewish to wear one. As you knit a Spiral Skullcap, reflect on the patterns of nature that are part of God's design.

The Spiral Skullcap: Encounter the "always there and everywhere" harmony of nature's spiral.

Experience It for Yourself

Spiral Skullcap

Materials: approximately 1 ounce of any weight yarn; use a variegated yarn or two colors that you alternate between sections to best see the effect of the spiral.

Needles: size appropriate to get a tight gauge with yarn.

Cast on 6 stitches.

Begin 6-row "Sections."

Note: To make 1: Lift "bar" before next stitch onto needle and knit into back.

Pattern for "Section"

Row 1: (begins at outer edge) Knit across approximately ⅔ of stitches (on first section, for example, 4 stitches). Turn.

Row 2: Knit back to outer edge.

Row 3: Knit approximately ½ of the remaining stitches (on first section, for example, 2 stitches). Turn.

Row 4: Knit back to outer edge.

Row 5: Knit across to inner edge.

Row 6a: If changing color, begin here. Knit to next to last stitch, make 1 (*see note*), knit last stitch (1 increased).

Note about approximating: You will not always be able to divide stitches exactly into thirds. Trust that whatever approximation you make will work. Still, you will probably enjoy coming to rows where the stitch number "resolves" into exact thirds.

Repeat the 6-row sections until row 6a measures 4½ inches across. At that point, continue knitting 6-row sections, *substituting row 6b for 6a.*

Row 6b: Knit 1, knit 2 together (1 decreased), knit to next to last stitch, make 1, knit last stitch (1 increased).

Repeat sections with 6b until diameter of semicircle measures approximately 8¼ inches at widest point.

Continue sections, substituting row 6c for 6b.

Row 6c: Knit 1, knit 2 together (1 decreased), knit across.

Continue these 6 rows until row 6c measures 2 inches wide. Knit section rows 1–5 and bind off.

Stitch together skullcap*:* Form into spiral, and pin to hold shape, over the rounded bottom of a 1½-pint Pyrex or similar bowl, first bending beginning of spiral. Begin stitching inside edges together, garter nub to garter nub (sometimes sewing two to one if necessary) until spiral is joined into circular shape. Make several stitches in ending to make smooth transition.

The beginning of the spiral is not at the center, but nearer an edge, like a seashell shape.

Wet thoroughly and block by patting into shape over the bowl. Let dry thoroughly.

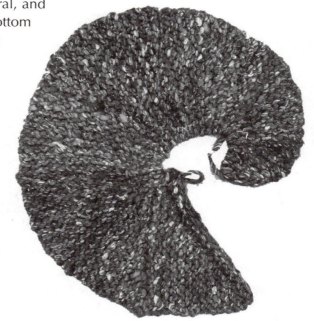

A skullcap as it comes off the needles, before sewing and blocking.

A Knitter's Link to Another Dimension

Knitting a simple band never fails to jolt my certitude that I live in a three-dimensional space. Scientifically, it's a topological shape called a Moebius band. Topology is a branch of mathematics that describes global (rather than local) shapes and their connectedness. Janna Levin, in *How the Universe Got Its Spots,* used the European concept of the world before 1492 to explain topology. The Europeans knew that, locally, the world had curves and bumpy mountains, but they feared that, globally, it was "flat," meaning "disconnected," or that there was an edge you could fall off. When you knit a Moebius band, it seems perfectly ordinary locally, exhibiting the usual two sides—face and back—at every stitch. As you knit round and round, however, you notice that you are creating a seemingly impossible global form that has only one continuous side and one continuous edge! When you look into the center space, you can see a continuous spiral forming.

Just a simple rotation after casting on leads you to pick up the base of the cast-on stitches. And then, after all the bases are picked up, knit the original cast-on stitches, as usual. This causes the inner and outer surfaces to merge—but you can't find the place they merge! Follow the band round and round. The fold moves. This isn't a magician's trick. I think it's God's little reminder of the fluid, paradoxical nature of life, a nudge out of limiting, "cut-and-dried" positions.

It's not surprising that this amazing twisted ring is the symbol used to indicate infinity and the cycles of nature. It can be seen in the orbits of particles in the Earth's geomagnetic tail and in the "virtual" path of the sun seen from earth over the course of the year, the analemma. The Moebius band inspired the original recycling icon (with an internal "negative" space that forms the primitive shape of a pine tree).

"One reason to knit mathematical objects," says Sarah-Marie Belcastro, "is to make visible their intrinsic geometry." In other words, we knitters have the power to bring concepts to "life." After I found "recipes" for knitting these wonders on various mathematicians' and knitters' sites on the Web, I couldn't get enough of them. I read later that August Ferdinand Moebius, the astronomer and mathematician who discovered the form in 1865, constructed it out of triangles. I experimented with knit/purl triangular shapes and started a smaller band than usual.

That night, Janice and I had our regular weekly meeting. She brought her project of the week—four different-but-related-and-sensational socks that she'll tell you about in chapter 5, "The Bearable Lightness of Knitting." I had the half-finished, possibly too small, neck warmer with me, but no new written pages to show her. I did, however have an exciting new concept—that the Moebius band could be "explained" by triangles. I had worked it out on a strip of paper on which I drew the triangles. It was true. When the band was connected in the ordinary way, the triangles weren't continuous, but after the half-twist they were. Only, when I showed it to Janice, I noticed that I had made a mistake in my big experiment of the week. The triangles I drew did not begin and end symmetrically. When I folded the strip to a point where they were symmetrical, the experiment had just the opposite result! I had nothing. All of my old insecurities came back in force and I felt as low as I could get. I really didn't think I was capable of ever finding spiritual meaning, let alone writing this book, or for that matter, ever knitting something worthwhile.

Happily, my work on the Knitting Way had actually changed what I could do with those miserable internal messages, in contrast to my old ways. Still moving along with the ebbs and flows of life, the next morning I sat down with the band and decided to keep going. After all, the triangles were continuous on the piece, even though I had proved on paper that it wouldn't work. I decided to increase on this piece rather than start again. The increase created an attractive drape, not the dismal picture I had of the project (and of myself) the night before. It worked as a neck cozy and headband, and the way it draped made me try it on a doll to see how it worked as a shawl. I liked it.

This happened at a time I was having major trouble writing this chapter, and it provided the break I needed. Knitting a big band to cuddle around my own blocked, spiritual-seeker shoulders was an enticing project just then, especially since I was about to be the passenger on a six-hour car trip each way to my mother's ninetieth birthday party in Maryland. I swatched a couple of yarns from my stash and, after a soul-searching encounter with myself, decided on using a yarn I had in a sweater quantity (a sweater that I had actually planned) although I would only be using a half-sweater's worth. The triangles really showed up well with this yarn, I had faith in the project (and no time to go to the yarn shop), and that was what was important right then.

Heading out on the trip the next morning, I found a triangle pattern, which made up the walls of the hexagonal sanctuary of Bet Shalom Synagogue in Minnetonka, Minnesota, in a newspaper article that I had clipped out months ago. Now I noticed it was actually a fractal pattern of triangles within triangles.

Achieving the new pattern was worth ripping out some of the rounds I had already knit (on four hundred stitches), and it gave me a chance to check out the width around my shoulders before I put the stitches back on the needles. I have to say, putting the stitches back on a Moebius strip is another way to experience the wonders of the form—and this was not the only time I had to rip back on this project. It is wonderfully engaging, requiring and deserving the knitter's attention, yet my old habit of drifting off still haunts me, and when I come back to the present I may find myself off a stitch.

I just couldn't (and still can't) get over how the triangles form a continuum—a pattern that's completely continuous, symmetrical, and reversible—on what I wound up calling the Wonder Wrap. It wasn't until I got home that it dawned on me that Moebius used actual triangle shapes to form his band, not a rectangular piece of paper marked out with triangles. Duh! Once again, I had missed information hidden in plain sight. When I snipped off the ends of the paper to the angle of the sides of the end triangles, lo and behold the paper model demonstrated the principle.

I bound off, praying it would work. It gave me the hug I needed, along with some more information. It said, "Two more rounds of triangles, please, and work the last triangles on smaller needles." Back on the needles it went. The Wonder Wrap works as a shawl and a poncho, a shawl-collared scarf and a hooded scarf, and the Mini Wrap works as a collar/neck cozy and a headband—each with infinite possibilities of contour and drape. The Mini Wrap is a good place to start. I share the patterns with love.

As you experience knitting these mind-opening shapes, imagine other wondrous possibilities waiting to be recognized.

Experience It for Yourself

Mini Wrap (Wonder Wrap)

Mini Wrap Materials: Worsted weight yarn (I used one 50-gram ball of an unidentifiable yarn from my stash) [or bulky weight yarn: I used the better part of one 100-gram skein].

Needles: 29- to 32-inch size US 9, or the shortest length circular that is manageable to knit with when the coil wraps around twice, *in the size to get gauge*.

Gauge: 4.5 stitches equals 1 inch [bulky, 3.5 stitches equals 1 inch].

Mini Wrap: Begin with a small step to see things in a new way.

Wonder Wrap Materials: Worsted weight yarn (I used 9 balls of Aurora 8, which has 98 yards each).

Needles: 32- to 60-inch circulars US 8 and US 6 or size to get gauge.

Gauge: 5 stitches equals 1 inch.

The instructions are given for the *Mini Wrap* (with the instructions for the *Wonder Wrap* following in parentheses).

Wonder Wrap: A reminder of the wondrous possibilities all around you.

With long-tail method, cast on 60 (200) stitches. Instead of joining in a circle by knitting into the first stitch, rotate the stitches downward and knit into back loop of the first stitch's "base." Continue around, knitting into the back loop at the base of each stitch. When you've picked up the 60 (200) stitch bases, you'll be back at the first stitch. Place a marker. Continue knitting around on the original cast-on stitches. Place another color marker. [120 (400) stitches]

Pattern Stitch

Note: To knit "Round," work past first marker and then around to second marker. It will seem like two rounds, but is the same round being knit from one side of the cast-on edge and then from the other, forming the amazing one-sided, one-edged band.

Round 1: *Purl 1, knit 8, purl 1. Repeat from * around.

Round 2: *Purl 2, knit 6, purl 2. Repeat from * around.

Round 3: *Purl 3, knit 4, purl 3. Repeat from * around.

Round 4: *Purl 4, knit 2, purl 4. Repeat from * around.

Round 5: Purl around.

Round 6: Knit around.

Round 7: *Knit 4, purl 2, knit 4. Repeat from * around.

Round 8: *Knit 3, purl 4, knit 3. Repeat from * around.

Round 9: *Knit 2, purl 6, knit 2. Repeat from * around.

Round 10: *Knit 1, purl 8, knit 1. Repeat from * around.

Round 11: Purl around.

Round 12: Knit around. (On *Mini Wrap,* increase on this round as directed in increase step.)

For *Wonder Wrap,* repeat these 12 rounds (as defined in **Note**) of *Pattern Stitch* one more time, ending after round 11. For the *Mini Wrap* I didn't repeat, but ended after round 11.

20	19	18	17	16	15	14	13	12	11	10	9	8	7	6	5	4	3	2	1	Round
I	I	I	I	I	I	I	I	I	I	I	I	I	I	I	I	I	I	I	I	12
—	—	—	—	—	—	—	—	—	—	—	—	—	—	—	—	—	—	—	—	11
I	—	—	—	—	—	—	—	—	I	I	—	—	—	—	—	—	—	—	I	10
I	I	—	—	—	—	—	—	I	I	I	I	—	—	—	—	—	—	I	I	9
I	I	I	—	—	—	—	I	I	I	I	I	I	—	—	—	—	I	I	I	8
I	I	I	I	—	—	I	I	I	I	I	I	I	I	—	—	I	I	I	I	7
I	I	I	I	I	I	I	I	I	I	I	I	I	I	I	I	I	I	I	I	6
—	—	—	—	—	—	—	—	—	—	—	—	—	—	—	—	—	—	—	—	5
—	—	—	—	I	I	—	—	—	—	—	—	—	—	I	I	—	—	—	—	4
—	—	—	I	I	I	I	—	—	—	—	—	—	I	I	I	I	—	—	—	3
—	—	I	I	I	I	I	I	—	—	—	—	I	I	I	I	I	I	—	—	2
—	I	I	I	I	I	I	I	I	—	—	I	I	I	I	I	I	I	I	—	1

Chart for pattern stitch. (Key: | represents knit; — represents purl.)

Increase: On round 12 of the last repeat, *increase in the first stitch and in the tenth. Repeat from * around, where "the first stitch" refers to the first stitch of each triangle base. [144 stitches (480 stitches)]

Pattern Stitch after Increase

Round 1: *Purl 1, knit 10, purl 1. Repeat from * around.

Round 2: *Purl 2, knit 8, purl 2. Repeat from * around.

Round 3: *Purl 3, knit 6, purl 3. Repeat from * around.

Round 4: *Purl 4, knit 4, purl 4. Repeat from * around.

Round 5: *Purl 5, knit 2, purl 5. Repeat from * around.

Round 6: Purl around.

Round 7: Knit around.

Round 8: *Knit 5, purl 2, knit 5. Repeat from * around.

Round 9: *Knit 4, purl 4, knit 4. Repeat from * around.

Round 10: *Knit 3, purl 6, knit 3. Repeat from * around.

Round 11: *Knit 2, purl 8, knit 2. Repeat from * around.

Round 12: *Knit 1, purl 10, knit 1. Repeat from * around.

24	23	22	21	20	19	18	17	16	15	14	13	12	11	10	9	8	7	6	5	4	3	2	1	
I	I	I	I	I	I	I	I	I	I	I	I	I	I	I	I	I	I	I	I	I	I	I	I	14
-	-	-	-	-	-	-	-	-	-	-	-	-	-	-	-	-	-	-	-	-	-	-	-	13
I	-	-	-	-	-	-	-	-	-	-	I	I	-	-	-	-	-	-	-	-	-	-	I	12
I	I	-	-	-	-	-	-	-	-	I	I	I	I	-	-	-	-	-	-	-	-	I	I	11
I	I	I	-	-	-	-	-	-	I	I	I	I	I	I	-	-	-	-	-	-	I	I	I	10
I	I	I	I	-	-	-	-	I	I	I	I	I	I	I	I	-	-	-	-	I	I	I	I	9
I	I	I	I	I	-	-	I	I	I	I	I	I	I	I	I	I	-	-	I	I	I	I	I	8
I	I	I	I	I	I	I	I	I	I	I	I	I	I	I	I	I	I	I	I	I	I	I	I	7
-	-	-	-	-	-	-	-	-	-	-	-	-	-	-	-	-	-	-	-	-	-	-	-	6
-	-	-	-	-	I	I	-	-	-	-	-	-	-	-	-	-	I	I	-	-	-	-	-	5
-	-	-	-	I	I	I	I	-	-	-	-	-	-	-	-	I	I	I	I	-	-	-	-	4
-	-	-	I	I	I	I	I	I	-	-	-	-	-	-	I	I	I	I	I	I	-	-	-	3
-	-	I	I	I	I	I	I	I	I	-	-	-	-	I	I	I	I	I	I	I	I	-	-	2
-	I	I	I	I	I	I	I	I	I	I	-	-	I	I	I	I	I	I	I	I	I	I	-	1

Chart for pattern stitch after increase.

Round 13: Purl around.

Round 14: Knit around.

For the *Wonder Wrap*, I repeated these 14 rounds of *Pattern Stitch after Increase* one more time. For the *Mini Wrap* I didn't repeat and ended after round 12. If your ball of yarn is running out before round 12, you can end after completing an earlier round to leave enough yarn for bind-off.

Mini Wrap: Bind off. (*Wonder Wrap*: Change to smaller needles and repeat 14 rounds of *Pattern Stitch after Increase* one more time through round 12. Bind off.)

Deeper into the Mystery

After I tried the Moebius construction, I wanted to go deeper into the mystery. There's a higher dimensional structure—with only one side that's both the inside and outside—called a "Klein bottle," conceived by the German mathematician Felix Klein at the end of the nineteenth century. I read that joining two Moebius strips can create it. Four dimensions are actually needed, so we have to fudge a little in the three-dimensional space we recognize by leaving a hole for the inside and outside to pass through—on their way to becoming the outside and the inside. It makes a fabulous hat that we call "the Hat of Infinite Possibility," since it can be transformed into an ever-changing variety of shapes and color patterns (if each

Moebius strip is a different color) by working with its emerging inside-outside configurations. Because it's not locked in an either/or fixation, the Hat of Infinite Possibility contains the whole universe. Do you see a lesson here?

If, when you knit the Wonder Wraps, you had trouble imagining other wondrous possibilities waiting for you to recognize, here's another project that will take you deeper into the mystery.

Hats of Infinite Possibility: Be drawn into the Mystery as you draw one of the hats into itself.

Experience It for Yourself

Hat of Infinite Possibility

Knit two Moebius bands, which you will sew together to form the Hat of Infinite Possibility. They can be two Mini Wraps of different colors, which will fit a child's head at 4.5 stitches to an inch, or make the Mini Wraps in a larger gauge or add another repeat (through round 5) for an adult size. You can also use Moebius bands of different stitch patterns and/or different yarns with different gauges knit with the same number of stitches for ease in joining. Each combination creates a unique hat.

To see how your particular combination will work as a hat, with a yarn needle and a length of yarn long enough to stitch around a complete edge, begin basting the edges, close to the edge, of one band to another. Continue around. You will find it necessary to stop when there is still an

opening left of a couple of inches, since you are creating a four-dimensional object within three-dimensional constraints. Play with the shape, by drawing the hat into itself. Isn't it fun! There's literally no end, since the inside and the outside are one side. If you like this combination, sew together with more permanent stitching, if you wish.

Social Science Comes In

Spirituality and religiousness are gaining increasing attention as factors that affect an individual's health. A 1995 meeting at the National Institutes of Health, cosponsored by the National Institute of Aging and the Fetzer Institute, established the need for a meaningful, coherent, and consistent measure of spirituality. At the outset there was a clarifying statement distinguishing between religiousness and spirituality: "Spirituality is concerned with the Transcendent, addressing ultimate questions about life's meaning, with the assumption that there is more to life than what we see or fully understand. Spirituality can call us beyond self to concern and compassion for others. While religions aim to foster and nourish the spiritual life—and spirituality is often a salient aspect of religious participation—it is possible to adopt the outward forms of religious worship and doctrine without having a strong relationship to the Transcendent." However, the Dalai Lama says that religion is a vital bridge. In Janice's view the Transcendent desires to reach us through a bridge of relationship. Knitting and prayer time is when we listen to the Transcendent trying to get to us. It's not just a one-way conversation. Using our knitting as the space for the conversation to take place is the art of the Knitting Way.

Daily spiritual experience was an aspect that had never been fully addressed, despite its reported importance in people's lives and its potential connection to health, according to researcher Lynn G. Underwood, PhD, who developed a measurement tool called the Daily Spiritual Experience Scale (DSES). "The DSES assesses features that ... pass through the core of the person to affect physical and mental health, social and interpersonal interactions, and functional abilities," she writes. Underwood, in her interviews with subjects, found connection to be an important concept. "Western spirituality emphasizes a personal connection with God, whereas Eastern and Native American spirituality, for example, place more emphasis on a connection with all of life and on connection as being part of a greater whole." We'll go deeper into how knitting addresses all these core areas later in this book.

The perception of a supportive interaction with the Transcendent is measured through feelings of strength and comfort; divine love; and expectation of divine intervention or inspiration. The DSES is intended to measure your perception of—and interaction with—the Transcendent, however you define it. And here's another paradox. You don't have to believe in the Transcendent to encounter it. Ideas and beliefs don't bring understanding. Honoring and participating in the craft of life does.

To gauge where your experience of connection is right now, try answering the questions posed by the Daily Spiritual Experience Scale.[5]

Experience It for Yourself

The Daily Spiritual Experience Scale

The list that follows includes sixteen items, which you may or may not experience. Consider how often you directly have this experience, and try to disregard whether you feel you should or should not have these experiences. A number of items use the word *God*. If this word is not a comfortable one for you, please substitute another idea, which calls to mind the Divine or Holy for you. Record the number from 1 to 5 that best reflects your experience for each statement: (1) many times a day, (2) every day, (3) most days, (4) once in a while, (5) never or almost never.

1. I feel God's presence.
2. I experience a connection to all life.
3. During worship, or at other times when connecting with God, I feel joy, which lifts me out of my daily concerns.
4. I find strength in my religion or spirituality.
5. I find comfort in my religion or spirituality.
6. I feel deep inner peace or harmony.
7. I ask for God's help in the midst of daily activities.
8. I feel guided by God in the midst of daily activities.
9. I feel God's love for me, directly.
10. I feel God's love for me, through others.
11. I am spiritually touched by the beauty of creation.
12. I feel thankful for my blessings.
13. I feel a selfless caring for others.
14. I accept others even when they do things I think are wrong.
15. I desire to be closer to God.
16. In general, how close do you feel to God on a scale from 1–5 (with 1 the closest)?

Now add your recorded numbers together. The lower your score, the greater your daily spiritual experience.

Wherever you are in your daily spiritual experience, your path has led you to the Knitting Way. We hope you'll come with us on our journey to a place beyond words.

3 Sacred Space

Your Knitting as an Opening and a Sanctuary

Space between the Loops

A Safe Space for Contemplation

All creation has a beginning and a path. So it is with knitting.

> *In the Beginning there was Formlessness, then*
> *Rhythm, then the Directions:*
> *The Horizontal, the Vertical, the Diagonals, the Top,*
> *the Bottom, the Left, the Right.*
>
> *And Rhythm knew the Directions and begat the*
> *Curve.*
> *And the Curve knew Rhythm and begat the Wave,*
> *and the Spiral, and the Loop.*
>
> *And the Loop became the Circle, and the Circle*
> *begat Space.*
> *And Space was manifest and embraced all Forms*
> *and Formlessness.*
>
> *And all else followed: "Like Nature."*
>
> —Julio Mateo[1]

Knitting is not just something you do, it is a place that you can go. The mind needs a safe and secure place for thoughts and dreams—a place of resting that settles the spirit and refreshes the brain. Knitting can do that. Opening yourself to this aspect of knitting can be full of surprises—most pleasant, some revealing. When I knit, the rhythm of my hands and needles creates space in my mind, which opens up the focus of my thoughts, much like riding on a train where the clickety clack of the wheels on the track sends us into contemplation. This kind of focus allows for meaningful meditative moments. Knitting can be a partner in prayer and contemplation, a sanctuary of space.

How often we just knit away, not even looking at the flow from our hands. Taking time to observe this phenomenon that we call knitting can do wonders for our work and for our souls. It's amazing that this line, this ray becomes sculpted fabric. Loops, bumps, color, smoothness, roughness are all formed from one line, joined together as the construction material for countless objects of beauty and utility.

Every stitch, every loop is a thing of beauty all by itself, unique and important in the final outcome. (Just as we are.) Touching the loops all around it, having a little space inside it, the stitch is a soldier lined up awaiting orders and at the same time acting independently to bring its own quality to the work. Is the stitch open or closed? Is the stitch elastic or rigid? Does the stitch cooperate with its brothers and sisters in the row or does it go its own way, leaning left or right? Remember to stop and take in with your eyes and your hands how your piece is acting. Take joy in that and accept what it brings to itself.

I noticed in a piece that I am working on that even though I am working back and forth in rows, the fabric has a vertical feel to it. All the little Vs of the knit side of stockinette stitch appear to run up and down. Is this a paradox? Don't we move along the horizontal to find our way to the vertical? Like geese flying south or the veins of a leaf, this "V inside V" is a soothing thing to me. Some people think these stitches look like tiny hearts. That's a nice image, too. Heart over heart over heart, each vertical is a tower of the love for the knitting, its final destination, and the heart of the creator.

And what shall we think of purl? Is this the knit stitch standing backward, its face away from the knitter, a naughty child in the corner? Is it the reason for that misbehaving curl of stockinette? Is that why we so often call the purl side the wrong side? Or do I misjudge this purl? It *is* uniquely suited to its place in the fabric, playing an important role to the elastic end and shining as the star of reverse stockinette stitch. If the purl stitch is the knit stitch backward, then is the knit stitch the purl stitch backward? Maybe there really are two different sides of the same coin. Do you envision these things in your own knitting?

How do you see the tiny stitches of your life? How closely do you look at them? Feelings, longings, character, soul—do we look closely or do we say, "Yes, yes, feelings, longings, etcetera. So what?" Knitting gives us an opportunity to slow down enough to look at and accept the deepness of ourselves, our inside places that wait to meet us there, to show us truth. It gives us the time to examine and contemplate. Looking—seeing the uniqueness, the depth, the soul-transforming truth—is a worthy goal.

The beyond is not what is infinitely remote, but what is nearest at hand.

—Dietrich Bonhoeffer

When I was in my thirties, my brother-in-law pointed out that I didn't look at my hands when I worked. Until then I hadn't noticed that I was in the habit of looking in the other direction. This was true when I washed dishes or folded laundry and when I knitted. Could it be that part of the reason I enjoyed knitting so much was that I didn't have to look at what I was doing? It was only when I started writing this book, thirty years later, that I was compelled to take a good look at what was right in front of me. When I pointed my eyes in the direction of my knitting, I only saw what I expected to see. I was a "professional," after all. I had a working knowledge of a fabulous array of techniques for everything from casting on to binding off, picked up from a library of books and videos, myriad classes and retreats. I could even perform sweater surgery.

Still, I had never made the effort to be there with my hands as they formed each knit and purl, so I had really made only a half-hearted connection with my beloved craft of over fifty years. Giving attention to what's nearest at hand is another gift of the Knitting Way. I never realized so much was going on in the world of stitches I was creating with my hands as I absentmindedly knitted.

The Yin and Yang of Knitting

A description of knitting by Mary Thomas in *Mary Thomas's Book of Knitting Patterns* has a rather biblical aura, I think, reminiscent of the book of Genesis: "Knitting begins with one foundation fabric, and from this all patterns originate. This fabric has two names, because it has two views, a FRONT [face] and a BACK. The front is known as Knit Fabric, commonly called Stocking [or stockinette] while the back is known as Purl [or reverse stockinette] Fabric."[2]

So, Purl (the Adam of knitting) and Knit (the Eve) are two sides of the same stitch "so opposite as black and white in every characteristic." Every Purl has a Knit side. Every Knit has a Purl side. We can experience this great truth of the universe every time we knit: Every opposite is part of a whole system, like night and day, male and female, life and death, conscious and unconscious, good and bad, active and passive, space and time. One does not exist without the other.

"Every pattern of thought must have its reverse side ... [I] widen my attention enough to view the irreconcilable opposites both together and realize that neither extreme could represent all the faces," observed Marion Milner, a writer, artist, and psychotherapist. As a young woman in the 1930s, Milner spent seven years doing "spiritual detective work" detailed in an eye-opening book called *A Life of One's Own* (originally written under the pen name Joanna Field). She warned of accepting the superiority of male objective reasoning, "a narrow focus mode that sees everything as a means to an end making contentment always in the future," over female subjective intuition. "What's required," Milner discovered, "is recognition of the value of both male and female attributes and of their presence in all of us."[3] Like the yin and yang of ancient Eastern philosophy, this complementary ideal can be applied to knitting.

Knit and Purl each have their characteristic natures. Knit provides a vertical line of design and Purl creates a horizontal; each has its own peculiar elasticity and variation in depth and width. A garment in stockinette stitch, if worn with the purl side out, is slightly shorter and broader than when worn with the knit side out, because the stitches take the opposite bend when encircling the body. So in one fabric there can be two different elastic pulls!

Mind-opening, isn't it? It's interesting to note that French mathematician Henry Poincaré, whose keen observations germinated into chaos theory (the recognition of meaningful patterns in the seeming chaos of nature), "unvented" purling as a young man after carefully observing a knitting woman's hands while he was on a stroll. After pondering the movements of her hands as he walked, he excitedly rushed back to tell her how to create the stitch's polar opposite. "Unventing" is the term that Elizabeth Zimmermann, the knitting guru whose story we'll delve into later on, used in humble homage to the wisdom that had come before her when she discovered a technique in knitting.

Stocking and Garter: A symbol of the balance of "opposites" that creates harmony in knitting and life. (Reprinted from *Mary Thomas's Book of Knitting Patterns.*)

The synergy between the knit and purl polarity makes for dynamic possibilities. In a ribbing pattern (knit 2, purl 2, etc.), knits stand out boldly in a vertical line and purls recede because they are facing the other way. The opposing action of knits and purls creates a widthwise elastic pull, which causes the fabric to pull *in*.

In garter stitch (every row knit) one row shows the back of all the stitches and one row the front. The purl row stands out boldly in a horizontal line, while knit stitches recede to the background. The opposing action of knits and purls creates a depthwise elastic pull, which causes the fabric to pull *up*.

A fabric that combines both vertical and horizontal lines has a two-way stretch, so it is balanced. This is the key to knitting, and to the life of a knitter. As Mary Thomas reminds us, a "simple picture memory of the Vertical and Horizontal principles of Knitted Fabric is aptly supplied in the 'Stocking and the Garter,' which was hung as a Trade Sign over the door of a professional knitter's home or workshop."[4]

Reflect on the possibilities, and the importance of balance, in your world as you explore how a small sampling of possible knit/purl combinations changes the world of knitted fabric.

Experience It for Yourself

Cast on 20 stitches and knit a ribbing sampler by working each of the following ribs.

Rib 1: Knit 1, purl 1 across for 18 rows.

Rib 2: Knit 2, purl 2 across for 18 rows.

Rib 3: Decrease one stitch at beginning and end of next row to accommodate 6-stitch repeat of knit 3, purl 3 across for 18 rows.

Rib 4: Increase 1 stitch at beginning and end of next row to bring stitch count back to 20: Row 1: knit 3, purl 2 across; Row 2: knit 2, purl 3 across. Repeat rows 1 and 2, eight more times (18 rows).

Rib 5 (a variation of "mistake" rib): Row 1: Knit 1, purl 1 across; Row 2: Knit across. Repeat rows 1 and 2, eight more times (18 rows).

Bind off.

Then, cast on 20 stitches, and see what happens when you arrange the knits and purls differently to form what are called "welt" patterns (because the purl ridges appear raised like welts).

Welt 1 (four-row repeat): *Purl across, knit across, knit across, purl across. Repeat from * 3 more times, then purl across, knit across (18 rows).

Welt 2 (six-row repeat): *Purl across, knit across, purl across, purl across, knit across, purl across, repeat from * two more times (18 rows).

Welt 3 (four-row repeat): *Knit 5, purl 5 across for two rows, purl 5, knit 5 across for two rows, repeat from * three more times; ending with two rows of knit 5, purl 5 (18 rows).

Welt 4 (fourteen-row repeat): Knit across, purl across, knit across, purl across, knit across for three rows, purl across, knit across, purl across, knit across for two rows, purl across, knit across. Work first four rows again (18 rows).

At the end of this swatch strip, try a "garter welt," so famous for fooling people with its indecipherable construction, according to Mary Thomas, that it has earned many names around the world such as Puzzle Stitch, Wager Welt, and All Fool's Welt.

Welt 5 (Puzzle Stitch, eight-row repeat): *Knit across, purl across, knit 6 rows, repeat two times (24 rows). Bind off.

> What goings-on in each sampler! How different they are. Isn't it remarkable how you were able to change the fabric "story" of a particular yarn? Trace how the stitch patterns transform into one another. Can you tell the difference between the front of the fabric and the back? Just a small change can make a difference!

Space between the Loops
The Shape of the Loop

The shape of the loop seems simple but in fact it is not. The loop has not always existed. It has to begin at some point, when a straight line suddenly leaves its course.… Loop motion is described not only by space … but also by [time].… There is always a "before" and an "after," an interval between "not yet" and "not anymore," between "it was" and "it is now."

—Janez Strehovec, "Text as Loop"[5]

How deceptively we see the loops of our knitting. What are they? Do we really know them?

Now, here's the Puzzle Stitch riddle: Looking at your swatch of knitting, and without peeking at the instructions you followed, how many purl rows are there in Welt 5? To check if you were correct, look at the Puzzle Stitch Pattern again.

Drawing on the Connection

The knit loops on the face side of stockinette when viewed after a 180-degree turn of the piece transform into the spaces between the loops that had been the spaces *(and still are)* from the original viewpoint. Something to ponder, almost like a koan. A koan, in Eastern philosophy, like the space between the loops, is a question that has no apparent answer but contains "patterns, like blueprints, for various inner exercises in attention … enabling the individual to hold entire universes of thought in mind all at once," according to Thomas Cleary in *Instant Zen—Waking Up in the Present.* Koans such as the famous "What is the sound of one hand clapping?" are resolved rather than answered.

When I read Betty Edwards's *Drawing on the Right Side of the Brain,* one of her statements particularly intrigued me.

She said, "Drawing gives one a feeling of power—not power over things or people, but some strange power of understanding or knowing or insight. Or perhaps it is just the power of connection itself." I decided to draw stockinette knitting, working from Edwards's basic strategies of perception. In terms of stockinette, this meant that I had to pay attention to: (1) the edges, where one stitch ends and another begins; (2) the negative spaces and how they define the stitches; (3) the relationships and proportions of the stitches to one another and the whole fabric; (4) what part is visible and what is hidden at the moment; (5) the "suchness" of the fabric that makes it "what it is and none other."

I found this drawing to be a difficult challenge. Apparently, I did not have as clear a perception of the stitch structure as I thought I had.

Experience It for Yourself

Photocopy the dotted grid on this page and try your hand at drawing plain stockinette knitting.

To help you out, here's a point of reference: "Each stitch has a top arc (head), two legs, and two bottom half arcs (feet). It is bound at the upper and lower ends … the head and the feet.… At the place where the legs transform into feet there are two points of contact with the previous stitch [in the row below].… If the feet of the stitch lie above [at the points of contact], and accordingly the legs below, then this is the … purl stitch.… If on the other hand, the bottom half arcs [feet] are below and the legs above, then this is the technical front

61

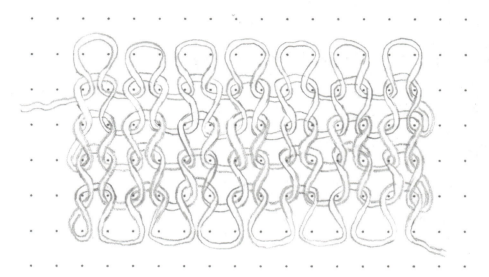

Can you imagine the spaces between the loops becoming the stitches when you turn your drawing upside down?

of the stitch [knit]." At least, that's how stockinette is described in "The Principles of Knitted Structures" of the University of Manchester (England) Institute of Science and Technology Department of Textiles.

Quantum Knitting

When drawing the stitches, I was astounded to discover that a knitted loop is a loop only through its relationship with the stitch in the previous row. In its own row the yarn travels in a path that's really a rhythmic wave. Oh! So that's why the stitches will zip out, right across—in either first-stitch-to-last or last-stitch-to-first direction—when you snip the yarn of just one stitch, and why they'll unravel down the fabric at a rate facilitated or impeded by the nature of the yarn.

The stitch is both wave and loop. It depends on how you look at it. Like the paradoxical particle/wave nature of the electron, the answer to whether a stitch is a wave or a loop is "yes." Something to reflect on as we knit.

The edge (selvedge) stitches have a different nature just because of their place in the path, which is the place where the wave of that row begins or ends. The edge stitches serve as connectors between the past row and the future row, making them look and behave like a crocheted chain. They have a vertical purl "bump" on their back side because the working yarn travels *up or down* between stitches from one row to the next rather than following the knit stitch's usual wavy path to the next stitch in the row.

The edge stitches, like a crocheted chain, unravel beautifully down from last-stitch-to-first-stitch direction, but any attempt to unravel them in the opposite direction makes them tighten like a noose around the next stitch in the chain. When unraveling in the direction of first stitch to last, instead of pulling the yarn to zip an end stitch out (which causes an ouch!), you must pick the end of the yarn out through the stitch before it will let you proceed to the next row. It's not really a bully. It's just doing its job.

When I mentioned this to our friend Gway-Yuang (Karen) Ko, she immediately visualized that you would create a *square cord* by knitting a stockinette fabric of two stitches (so there would be only edge stitches). That's what comes of keenly observing the nature of things.

Experience It for Yourself

For a square cord, cast on two stitches and work 1 row knit, 1 row purl for as long as you like. To avoid turning after every 2-stitch row and also to make the process more interesting, try "knitting back backwards," the process I first learned by watching Meg Swansen, master knitter, publisher, and proprietor of Schoolhouse Press, and daughter of Elizabeth Zimmermann.

To knit back backwards, simply insert the left needle into the back of the first stitch on the right needle, wrap yarn around needle from left to right, and lift stitch over and off with the right needle. Joyce Williams, a disciple of Elizabeth Zimmermann and author of *Latvian Dreams*, says she teaches beginners to knit stockinette by knitting back backwards, but to avoid any preconceived notion of difficulty she calls it KOLN (knitting onto the left needle).

Hidden in Plain Sight

Optical illusions provide images that confuse the brain's preprogramming system because they provide more than one valid perception simultaneously. Betty Edwards, in *Drawing on the Artist Within,* says that these "ambiguous images provide experiences, at a conscious level, of the kind of shift necessary to grasp alternative perceptions." And the ability to understand alternative views is a gift of the Knitting Way.

Stockinette itself is an ambiguous image that can help us see things in new ways. Knitting is a fertile workshop for exploring negative space possibilities. Negative space is that space that bumps up against the outer edge of the object we see. The space between the fence posts, the places between the trees. If we only see the negative space, we will eventually see the object. Changing focus gives us a different perspective, which not only brings clarity, but actually brings a different experience—which expands our world.

Jar Heads: Can you change what you see?

Jar Heads

I tried graphing the famous Face/Vase illusion and wound up with a Face/Pet illusion. That's fine with me because I like animals! The Fair Isle pattern had to be knit in the round because the pattern had one solid color in each row that would leave the other color on the wrong end. Since I don't like working Fair Isle on the purl side, I decided to work the piece on single points using double knitting, and I tried

Beverly Royce's technique described in her book *Notes on Double Knitting*. I wanted to try the pattern out on a small piece, and with tassels added, it turned into a cute hat for my honey-spread jar. Janice wanted to run to the craft store to buy plastic eyes to glue on the jar. The idea of making other kinds of swatches into Jar Heads tickles my fancy.

This project takes concentration. It requires an intriguing technique and, at the end, there are two guys looking at one another. Or, is there just an animal in the middle? It depends on which we focus on—and a hint on how we shape our world.

Experience It for Yourself

Jar Head Illusion

Materials: Work with worsted or lighter weight yarn and appropriate needles. You will need approximately 20 grams each of a light and a dark color and small amount of a contrasting color.

One-Row Pattern Stitch: *Knit 1, and before removing stitch from left hand needle, slip 1. Repeat from * across. (Forms a double layer worked with the wrong side out.)

With contrasting color yarn, cast on 46 stitches. Work in Pattern Stitch for 2 rows, marking second row side with a safety pin. Break yarn leaving a few inches.

With light and dark color yarns, begin following chart (which shows the image upside

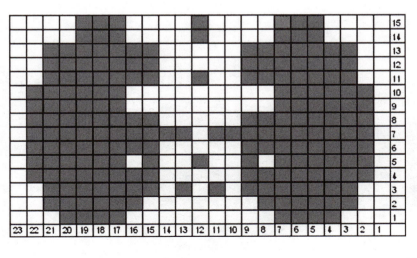

down, since you are working from the top of the cap down) continuing in Pattern Stitch.

On next row (the marked "shadow" side), repeat same row on chart that you worked on previous row, reversing colors. Always bring yarn around side of piece when you turn.

As you work, you face the inside of the piece, and the side you worked on the previous row. Repeat until chart is completed on both sides. Break yarns leaving a few inches and attach contrasting yarn. Work two rows in Pattern Stitch.

To separate the two layers to prepare for bind-off, transfer stitches, alternating between the other needle and an extra double pointed needle as follows: *First stitch to other needle, next stitch to extra needle. Repeat from * across. Break yarn, leaving 15 inches (enough for a sewn bind-off.)

Sewn Bind-Off: Thread tapestry needle with 15-inch end. Insert tapestry needle through second stitch from front to back and through first stitch from back to front. Insert tapestry needle into third stitch, from front to back and back through second stitch from back to front. Continue in this way across stitches on one needle, and continue across stitches on other needle. End off.

Da Vinci Message Seaman's Scarf: Hidden messages in knit and purl.

Da Vinci Knitting: Your Message Here

Leonardo da Vinci was a marvelous inventor. I sometimes wonder if this genius's mind ever turned off. Was he constantly thinking and creating, even in his sleep? Did he sleep? He was also a secretive man. Perhaps the religious climate of his time prompted the need for secrecy, but whatever the reason, da Vinci wrote a good portion of his notes in mirror writing, inscribing his letters backward from right to left. Held up to a mirror they were readable.

To further stretch our focus, we tried some knitted mirror writing, using welt patterns to form block letters. We knit our names into the fabric of scarves. It's interesting how the negative space helps form the letters. And, on the reverse side, there appears a mirror image. To the untrained eye, what we call da Vinci fabric has an interesting abstract design, particularly on the reverse side. What possibilities for your personal messages!

Example of the LINDA chart used to knit the Da Vinci Message Seaman's Scarf shown in the photo.

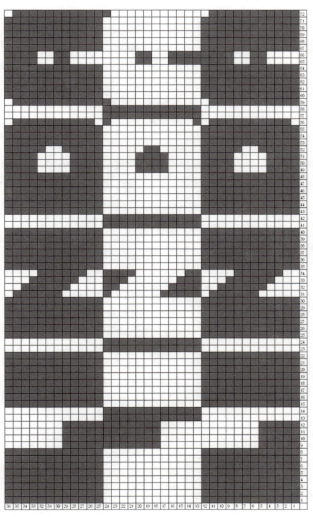

Experience It for Yourself

Da Vinci Message Seaman's Scarf

Materials: Heavy worsted weight yarn knit at a gauge of 4 stitches equals 1 inch; US 9 needles, or size to get gauge. A five-letter name scarf took 150 grams.

Letters are worked across width of scarf three times, alternating letters worked in knit with purl negative space and letters worked in purl with knit negative space. One possibility is to knit up the scarf with the purl letters in the middle between knit letters at the edges, switch to ribbing around neck, and knit back down with the purl letters at the edges and the knit letters in the middle.

Copy the letters from the alphabet chart on pages 208–209 to form the name or short message you wish to knit.

Cast on 42 stitches. Each edge of the scarf is worked by slipping the last three stitches at the end of each row, with yarn in front, and knitting the first 3 stitches at the beginning of each row. On the middle 36 stitches, work three repeats of a 12-stitch letter.

When name or message is complete, work in ribbing, as follows, for 17 inches: Slip 1 as if to purl, *knit 2, purl 2. Repeat from * across ending with purl 1.

Repeat your name or message chart. Bind off.

The Uninvited Guest

Feedback between tiny loops creates change, a healthy system according to *Seven Life Lessons of Chaos* by John Briggs and F. David Peat. Each of us exerts a subtle influence that together creates "butterfly" power, powerful but unpredictable. The image of a tsunami in Tokyo being caused by a butterfly flapping its wings in San Francisco represents the concept.

A closed system creates a limit cycle—an obsessive, repetitive loop—that leads to stagnation and death. That's why it's important to allow natural interactions and repetitions to proceed unimpeded. In these interactions and repetitions, simplicity and complexity constantly transform into one another, particularly during outbreaks of chaos. Order resumes when chaos reestablishes important feedback loops. *Seven Life Lessons of Chaos* tells us, "The unwelcome guest at the party challenges the normal order of our lives so we give more attention to nuances and subtle patterns." Dropped stitches and a break in the stitch are the uninvited guests at the knitting party. Let's have fun and invite them in!

Experience It for Yourself

Work a 20-stitch swatch in stockinette for several inches. Measure its dimensions and write them down. *Bind off 2, take a deep breath, and release the next stitch from the needle and drop it down to the cast-on edge, repeat from * 5 times. Measure the swatch again. Quite a change! Everything is still okay, and you've discovered a new fabric dimension. *Mary Thomas's Book of Knitting Patterns* has a delightful array of ladder motifs to frolic with. It's a chance to let go and take a leap—or a fall—and discover that you're still alive at the bottom! What's more, look at the new possibilities that open up before you. Maybe you were afraid to make a change in your life. Maybe you've been forced to make a change against your will and out of your control. This is a safe way to examine life's myriad possibilities.

Now, ready to snip a stitch in the middle of a swatch? After facing this uninvited guest, you'll be ready to fearlessly execute Elizabeth Zimmermann's "afterthought pocket or thumb." On a small stockinette swatch, decide where you want to annex and how many stitches wide you want the opening to be. Taking a deep, calming breath (it's so scary to use scissors on knitting), snip the center stitch and unravel both ways to the width of the opening you want. This is a good way to observe firsthand that you have one less stitch at the top of the opening (the stitches that were/are the spaces between the stitches) than at the bottom (which are simply the stitches, right now).

Finally, here's the process that may require lying down in a dark room, as Elizabeth Zimmermann suggested, playing the good mother in *Knitting Without Tears*. On a new swatch, mark the 3 center stitches. From the top of the swatch to the bottom, whip stitch (or crochet) the right leg of the stitch on the left together with the left leg of the middle stitch; then from the top to the bottom of the swatch, whip stitch (or crochet) the left leg of the stitch on the right with the right leg of the middle stitch. Then cut up through the center of the middle stitch. Voilà! You'll have *at the least*: (1) two swatches; (2) overcome a fear; and (3) learned a new way to create a cardigan. By the way, it's called "steeking."

Space between the Loops
I See Your True Colors Shining Through

In a town across the river from where I grew up, there was an old yarn shop. I remember, probably incorrectly, that it was in a white stucco building facing the river, and the store was always in disarray, with yarn everywhere in boxes and plastic bags. It was dingy and dusty and stale (read: cat urine) inside, but it was a place to get the different yarns and tools that could not be found in K-Mart. My mother and I crocheted and we found adventure in that old shop. An old woman owned the place and she sat right in the middle of the store space, in a ratty chair, knitting away. She was frumpy, eccentric, kind, and she kept cats (hence the cat urine). It was the kind of place that entered my imagination, rattled around, and cogitated until knitting found me. Color and texture just jumbled everywhere like artist's paint on a palette halfway through a painting.

I love color. I really love color. I never met a color I didn't like. I am thankful for colors—their beauty, their fire, their ice. Color is a massive presence in my knitting. The yarn palette is like the difference between Crayola's ninety-six-crayon box and the eight-crayon box.

How do you see the colors of your work? How many colors do you see in the world outside your window? Have you ever really looked at an ordinary, rough, hard rock from your garden? Do you think it is just gray or brown? Do you see the blush pinks and blues or the coppers, greens, and yellow ochre that paint its surface? How many yellows are in the sky? How many blues are in a rose? How many purples are found in a rusty wheelbarrow? How many greens are in the garden's soil?

I'm the first one to say, "When it comes to creativity, you don't have to follow the rules," so if you have your own sensibilities, don't let me change them. I know that many struggle when choosing colors for their projects. They are stymied and unsure and, sometimes, afraid. For the less than intrepid, I offer these very simple guidelines from basic color theory.

The primary colors are red, blue, and yellow. They are called "primary" because all other colors are made up of these (if you don't believe me, look at the color cartridge of your ink-jet printer). Think of them as the first generation. They are always happy to go along together no matter if they are all brights or all pastels. The secondary colors are orange, green, and purple. They are the second generation based on the marriages between red and yellow, yellow and blue, blue and red. They are always kind to each other, like the primaries. The tertiary colors are those colors created by the mixing of a primary with a secondary, for example, red plus orange makes red-orange, or orange-red, depending on the ratio of color mixed. They are the third generation, but it doesn't need to get that complicated. Now enters the complementary color. This is the color that, when played against its complement, brings out the better of each one. The complement of red is green (and vice versa). The complement of yellow is purple. The complement of blue is orange. Did you notice that the complement of a primary is a secondary made by the other two primary colors? These combinations "work" because of the interrelatedness of all colors. What a lovely mystery!

Part of that mystery is revealed by the reason we see colors. What we actually see is the reflection of the individual wavelength of each color from the spectrum (remember the rainbow?). When we look at a red shirt, the shirt isn't really red—what we see is the reflection of red's wavelength bouncing back to our eyes. The red shirt absorbs all of the other colors' wavelengths. This almost hurts the brain to think about. When we see the color white, we see all the colors reflecting back to us. When we see black we are seeing no reflections of wavelength, the total absorbency of wavelengths, the absence of color. I'm thankful God made the rainbow, a staple of children's drawings, a childlike gift of art, beauty, and love. In it lies the total explanation of color, but we are so exhilarated when we see a natural one that what we experience is awe. We don't need the explanation.

Cultivate an understanding of the warmness and coolness of colors. No matter what the color, if it reminds me of a sunrise, sunset, hot summer day, or Kansas wheat field, then it is warm. If it reminds me of the sea, breezes, rain forests, or snow, then it is cool. Blue may be hot, yellow may be cool. I realize that this is a very simplified idea, but it works for me. Usually, warm colors dance well together as do cool colors, but each can cut in on the other in quite a pleasant way. Color theory can all be explained in a much more scholarly and technical way, and it has been in many books and by many teachers. I'm happy to be simple.

Trust what you like; trust what you feel. Make a trip to your yarn shop, line up your stash, and spend some time with your new color friends. Lay them down next to each other and observe how they communicate with each other. Practice listening to how they whisper like lovers or scream like adversaries. Only by immersing yourself in their world, experiencing and accepting the characteristics of this gift of color, will you gain trust in what they can do and how you understand them.

Experience It for Yourself

You will need white paper, a ruler, a pencil, a small container of water, and the tray of a children's watercolor paint set. You may use plain printer paper and the brush that comes with the paint set, but a small investment in watercolor paper and a watercolor/natural hair brush (available at an art store or the art section of a craft store) will give you more control over the med-ium and more pleasing results.

On your paper mark out a 6-inch by 6-inch grid—36 1-inch squares. Across the top of the grid, write a heading over each column: red, yellow, blue, orange, green, purple.

Now with your paints, fill in every square in each column with the color listed at the top. Don't fill the square in all the way to the pencil line: Leave a little fence of white around your block of color. Allow the paint to dry completely. You will have six vertical red squares, six vertical yellow squares, and so on.

Back in Kansas with new vision!

On the left side of the grid, in front of each row, write: red, yellow, blue, orange, green, purple. Now repeat the filling in of every square in each horizontal row with the color stated at the left, all the way across, over the top of the previous colors now on your paper. You will create a color grid of blended colors that may surprise you.

Do you see the diagonal of your original colors running from the top left to the bottom right? Look at what happened to each combination and see if you can discern the parent colors in each block. Spend some time observing what is in front of you. This little exercise can open your eyes to see colors in a new way, and I think it is suitable for framing!

Visit www.theknittingway.com to see our color experiments in, well, color.

The Comfort Project

A knitting project itself can open up the "potential space" we all long for. Some traditional comfort projects are hats, socks, mittens, scarves, shawls, and simple sweater shapes, which, after they're "in your muscles" (we'll go into more about that in chapter 7, "Mind and Body"), coax you into a state of relaxation from which you can emerge better able to face the world. We became smitten with a traditional comfort project for quilters called Log Cabin Squares.

My quilt-as-you-knit version was something I had wanted to do since 1982. I just unearthed a now-out-of-print booklet called *Log Cabin Quilts,* by Bonnie Leman and Judy Martin, in which I had stashed some notes, diagrams, and a yellowed newspaper article by Ann Barry from the "Antiques View" column of the *New York Times*, Sunday, July 14, 1985, called "The Deft Geometry of Log-Cabin Quilts." I wasn't in much of a rush to explore, was I?

I relished each stitch of the puffy, perky, self-contained modules of Log Cabin Squares. Only knits, purls, and slip stitches were used. No sewing. Magic! Can you tell I love them? They cry out to be part of so many things—a quilt, a vest, a mat, a pillow top. The Cozy Tea Quilt I made with the squares keeps my tea hot for hours, but when my seven-year-old grandson, Jeremy, saw it he immediately put it on his head and managed to form a half-dozen different hat styles.

A buddy in my knitting group, Tomasina Schneider, kindly agreed to test some of the patterns in the book. Tomi's Log Cabin Squares opened a new dimension to the project. First of all, I realized how the personality of the knitter comes through in this little square. Knit of left-overs from other projects and oddballs lovingly collected, each square presents a picture of the knitter in the form of a small square. What depth is in that square! Then, Tomi decided to knit a solid-color square. In the photo on page 80, notice how different the spiral looks in the solid square than it does in the multicolored squares. It opens up new possibilities to explore. I love knitting!

Janice made the traditional structure her own with mitered-corner Log Cabin Squares that are small works of art. Each square is a dovetailed canvas painted with her "little paint pots" of yarn. She said that there is something about working with the two circular needles going and the traditional "dark, darker, darkest and light, lighter, lightest" quality that's satisfying to her soul.

There's a reason why Log Cabin Patterns are a time-honored classic among quilters (who also find them addictive, not ordinarily an indicator of spiritual health). For one thing, the squares automatically help you organize your stash (of yarn, in our case). Suddenly oddballs or scraps of yarn in your baskets or at the yarn store have new meaning—light, lighter, lightest and dark, darker, darkest—and will be smartly recruited for the squares. Variegated colors will call to you from the bottom of a bin.

The squares so neatly and logically build on themselves and relate to one another, in a Golden Ratio spiral, that you seem to have a partner in the project. They contain the knitting so pleasingly, a fence that holds thoughts and colors and decisions. Each strip rests waiting for the next, so happy to accept her sister when she comes. Playing with a layout to assemble them in a way that makes use of their diagonal light/dark halves is as much fun as knitting each square. The light/dark assembly combinations are endless.

Within the framework of these patterns, find a safe haven, a fenced-in place to rest and examine who you are inside.

Experience It for Yourself

Mitered-Corner Log Cabin Square

Materials: Choose yarns of near equal weight: 3 light colors, 3 dark colors, and 1 color for the center. I used 2-ply jumper weight Shetland wool on size US 4 circular needles and achieved a 6.5-inch square before blocking.

This square is made easier if you use 2 circular needles, 16 or 24 inches long. One will be a working needle and the other will act as a stitch holder when not working on its strip.

Note: *Make 1* in the instructions is accomplished by a backwards loop onto the right needle. Sometimes called an "e" cast-on.

With the color selected for the center square:

Cast on 10 and knit 20 rows in garter stitch (10 ridges). End with a wrong side (WS) row. Center square complete.

Begin Strip 1. All strips are 10 rows (5 ridges).

Row 1: With right side (RS) facing, knit 10 with light color A, make 1, and mark this just-created stitch. This will be the center stitch of the miter shaping. Rotate square ¼ turn to the right and pick up 10 stitches along the side of the center square—1 for each ridge (21 stitches on needle).

Row 2 and all even or WS rows: Knit.

Row 3: Knit 10, make 1, knit marked stitch, make 1, knit 10.

Row 5: Knit 11, make 1, knit marked stitch, make 1, knit 11.

Row 7: Knit 12, make 1, knit marked stitch, make 1, knit 12.

Row 9: Knit 13, make 1, knit marked stitch, make 1, knit 13.

End strip with row 10 (29 stitches on needle): Leave this needle holding the stitches.

Begin Strip 2: With RS facing, turn your work so that the strip just completed lies around the right and bottom of the center square. Cast-on edge of center square will be the top of your work now.

Row 1: With the second circular needle and dark color A, pick up 5 stitches across the 5 ridges at the end edges of strip 1. Pick up 10 stitches across the cast-on edge of center square make 1. Mark this just-created stitch. This will be the center stitch of the miter shaping. Rotate square ¼ turn to the right and pick up 10 stitches in the 10 ridges of left side of center square and pick up 5 stitches in the 5 ridges of strip 1 (31 stitches on needle).

Four mitered-corner Log Cabin Squares create a handsome work of art.

Row 2 and all even or WS rows: Knit.

Row 3 and all odd or RS rows: Knit to the marked stitch, make 1, knit the marked stitch, make 1, knit to the end of the row. Continue ending with row 10 (39 stitches on needle): Leave this needle holding stitches.

Begin Strip 3: Go back to first needle, with light color B.

Row 1: Pick up 5 stitches from the 5 ridges at the end edge of strip 2. Knit across to marked stitch, make 1, knit the marked stitch, make 1, knit to the end of the row (41 stitches on needle).

Row 2 and all even or WS rows: Knit.

Row 3 and all odd or RS rows: Knit to the marked stitch, make 1, knit the marked stitch, make 1, and knit across. Continue, ending with row 10 (51 stitches on the needle) Leave this needle holding stitches.

Continuing in the manner of Strip 3, and, alternating between needles, work with one and use the other as a stitch holder.

77

Strip 4: Use dark color B.

Strip 5: Use light color C. Bind off on row 10.

Strip 6: Use dark color C. Bind off on row 10. Weave in ends.

Options: Keep adding strips to make larger squares.

Log Cabin Quilted Square

Materials: A combination of worsted and DK weight yarns yielded 11 inch square on US 8 needles for me. 4 light colors, 4 dark colors, and 1 color for center (traditionally red for "heart and hearth" in a Log Cabin quilt).

With color selected for center square: Cast on 5 stitches.

Row A: Increase 1 stitch in each stitch across (10 stitches).

Row 1: *Knit 1, slip 1 (with yarn in front). Repeat across row. *Forms two layers.*

Rows 2–9: Repeat Row 1.

Row 10: *(with yarn in back) Slip 1, purl 1. Repeat across row. This adds a row to front layer.

Row 11: Repeat row 1.

Row 12: Repeat row 10. Front layer will have 4 more rows than back to "puff" after row 13.

Row 13: Knit 2 together, *knit 2 together, pass first stitch on right needle over last stitch and off needle. Repeat from * across.

1st Strip: With light color A, and right side facing you, pick up 5 stitches along top of center square. Repeat rows A–13.

Quilted squares.

2nd Strip: With light color A, and right side facing you, pick up 5 stitches along side of 1st strip and 5 stitches along side of center square (10 stitches). Repeat Rows A–13, working on 20 stitches.

3rd Strip: With dark color A, and right side facing you, pick up 5 stitches along side of 2nd strip, and 5 stitches along center square (10 stitches). Repeat Rows A–13, working on 20 stitches.

4th Strip: With dark color A, and right side facing you, pick up 5 stitches along side of 3rd strip, 5 stitches along center square, and 5 stitches along 1st strip (15 stitches). Repeat Rows A–13 working on 30 stitches.

5th Strip: With light color B, and right side facing you, pick up 5 stitches along side of 4th strip, 5 stitches along 1st strip, and 5 stitches along 2nd strip (15 stitches). Repeat Rows A–13, working on 30 stitches.

6th Strip: With light color B, and right side facing you, pick up 5 stitches along side of 5th strip, 10 stitches along 2nd strip, and 5 stitches along 3rd strip (20 stitches). Repeat Rows A–13 working on 40 stitches.

Repeat as established with 2 strips each of: dark color B, light color C, dark color C, light color D,

One Log Cabin quilted square forms a pillow cover by joining points at back of square.

Form a Cozy Tea Quilt with five Log Cabin quilted squares.

79

and dark color D, increasing number of stitches picked up by 5 on the second strip of each color. On last (16th) strip, pick up 45 stitches.

Run all ends to inside between quilted layers with tapestry needle.

Cozy Tea Quilt
Sew 5 Log Cabin Squares together to form bottomless cube. Leave opening in diagonal seams for spout and handle.

When I was trying to describe the attraction of being within the loop of such a project, I came across Sharon Plavnick's weblog at www.sharonstuff.typepad.com/knitknacks. Here she describes her love affair with the little basket-weave rectangles of entrelac knitting. The description so perfectly captured and expressed my feeling about the Log Cabin Squares that I asked Sharon if we could share it with you.

> Then, I was brought to my knees, humbled, laid low by the very condition I myself had been inflicting on others. I was in love, deep true devoted love. Now I was the slave, spending day and night with the object of my affection, my own wonderful love, my Entrelac Sweater. Instead of running around with any old scarf, hat, or slipper, I spent my time with this object only. It was a relief to just be myself with my true companion. No more decisions; no more hurting one to favor another; no more changing partners to fit the circumstances. No more turning my head at the flip of an eyelash, or the sparkle of novelty. I was content to spend loving time in the Garden of Noro [a hand-painted yarn], patiently nurturing each rectangle of love into a greater whole. It felt good to be so stable, so true, so patient with one another as we fell into the rhythm of our life together.

Julia Cameron in *The Artist's Way* describes why this is likely a positive obsession. "Looking at God's creation it is pretty clear that the creator itself did not know when to stop. There is not one pink flower, or even fifty pink flowers, but hundreds ... snowflakes, of course are the ultimate exercise in sheer creative glee. No two are alike. This creator looks suspiciously like someone who might send us support for our creative ventures."[6]

Experience It for Yourself

Knit in the dark.

Knit while blindfolded to see what is there while you visualize your way through the stitches.

Read the fabric with your fingers to recognize the pattern in loops and waves formed by your hands.

Watch through a mirror as your hands knit, and imagine yourself on the other side of the fabric.

Knit a swatch. Write down directions to reproduce the swatch. Follow directions and see what you missed.

Make believe this is your first time knitting. Experiment with hand positions, hold the needles and throw the yarn in an unfamiliar way, and so on.

4

Once Upon a Time

The Stories of Our Projects

The universe began as a story.... we are part human, part stories."

—Ben Okri, *Birds of Heaven*

It's said that Great Truths are passed on through stories. "Spirituality itself is conveyed by stories which use words in ways that go beyond words to speak the language of the heart," concluded Ernest Kurtz and Katherine Ketcham in their inspiring spiritual guide, *The Spirituality of Imperfection: Storytelling and the Search for Meaning.* But knitting stories *literally* do go beyond words because we can understand their meaning through the work of our hands. The stories that are passed down to us from the far reaches of the world transmit ways of being through the language of knitting—skills, concepts, patterns, guidelines, preferences, and possibilities—that we experience directly through our own expression of them.

There's a knitting culture transmitted through stories of knitters and knitting. This is a kind of infectious process that can be carried in many ways—in person, through books, videos, and now through the Internet—in other words, in any way that people find to convey and document how they've practiced the art of living in their own culture through this particular enthusiasm—what succeeded, what disappointed, where this led, what's the next challenge. Each of us tries things out for our own self and, so, contributes to the culture. Whenever one knitter meets another, the encounter perpetuates the culture. A knitter passing a fellow knitter on a park bench may not stop or even say a word, but she smiles, knowing that their common ground of knitting is solid under her feet. There is an intimacy there. This intimate sharing creates a River of Connection. It takes willingness and an immersion that's not easy for some of us.

The Internet, a new transmitter of the knitting culture, has added to the language, even coining nicknames for familiar concepts such as SABLE (Stash Accumulation Beyond Life Expectancy); KIP (Knitting in Public); UFO (Unfinished Object); and to communicate ripping out, tink (knit spelled backwards) and frog ("rip-it, rip-it"). Do any of these ring a bell? Discussion groups such as the Knitlist (www.knitlist.com), where these nicknames were coined, are as much about community as they are about knitting, and individual blogs, where knitters publicly journal their daily stories, bring everyone who's willing into the loop, sharing knowledge and discoveries, joys and disappointments.

The sense of a River of Connection felt by knitters may be responsible for the widespread belief that knitting has existed for as long as there have been sheep. It's hard to believe that knitting is relatively new. The ancient items discovered at archaeological sites that were thought to be knitted turned out to be netted, a looping method that's also called nail-binding, produced with a sewing needle. Until the past couple of hundred years, sweaters didn't even exist. Foot, leg, hand, and headgear were the knitted garments worn, and these weren't common until a few hundred years before sweaters. Men trained in guilds for years to develop the skill to produce the extremely fine, elaborate silk stockings highly regarded by the elite. But knitted socks, much comfier than the woven footwear previously worn, finally became so popular that women were able to supplement their income by knitting woolen socks. After knitting machines displaced the earning potential of hand-knit socks, men abandoned the craft, but women continued to knit for their families. There are various stories about why William Lee invented the knitting machine (most involving a woman spending more time knitting than enjoying his company, with his motive either revenge or rescue), but Queen Elizabeth I managed, during her lifetime, to prevent its use in the sixteenth century and kept the hand-knitting industry going for a while.

Richard Rutt, bringing the reader up to the events of 1987 in *A History of Hand Knitting*, wrote, "Socks and stockings were the most frequently hand-knitted garments from the beginning of popular knitting until the 1950s. Today they can hardly be seen, and only the old can remember how to turn a heel without referring to a book." However, he jumps to conclusions when he editorializes, "Stockings were always dull work. Today's knitter expects more pleasure from the craft."[1] I'm happy to say, as I write this, deep in the age of instant gratification, that the skill of turning a heel is coming back to our fingers, as one by one knitters find a place of rest in doing what may look "dull" on the surface. The River of Connection is flowing. If you haven't tried knitting socks, keep alert for knitters carrying double points and the glorious colors of sock yarns out there hoping that you'll notice. Don't forget to look at feet in sandals or clogs!

There are so many methods for knitting a sock it could make your head spin. Whole books have been written on the subject, and new variations keep cropping up. How do you decide which one to try? I arrived at sock knitting through my role at Patternworks, when I learned to knit a sock as part of the process of writing our basic sock pattern. There's something about the need to define a process that gives me the discipline, or the space, I need to work it through. The frame of the project itself isn't always enough. This is an insight about myself I owe to the process of writing this book.

The sock diagram in *Mary Thomas's Knitting Book* is the reason Janice can knit socks, and she always has a pair on the needles. As she says, "If you've never turned a heel, it doesn't seem as if it makes sense. But you keep going, in a leap of faith, and then, it's done and it's there, and you say to yourself 'Oh, I get it!' After knitting a zillion socks I know what's happening, but the sock's heel still says 'Ta dah' at the end. My advice: Trust what you're doing. It's only yarn and time." Most likely, you'll notice a particular technique when you're ready and approach knitting socks in the way you usually take on a new project. But that's another story.

Experience It for Yourself

Write a pattern for a sweater, or something else you'd like to knit to your own specifications. Give yourself the time, space, and opportunity to discover what you like. Keep a notebook to jot down ideas. Seek out similar items in the stores, on your friends, in the magazines and newspapers. Become intimate with these knits, when possible, by touching, trying on, measuring dimensions, counting stitches, and even weighing them to get an idea how much yarn you'll need. Study available patterns and keep notes on measurements, stitches per inch, recommendations of yarn type and amounts, needle size and techniques used. Become acquainted with different yarns and note their vital statistics. Be aware of the colors around you as you go through the day. Play with color combinations. Explore knitting techniques. Make swatches. Take your own measurements and record them. Learn to diagram a sweater.

Elizabeth Zimmermann's *Knitting Without Tears* for seamless sweaters and Cheryl Brunette's *Sweater 101* for basic styles with a front, back, and sleeves knit separately provide a helping hand. You'll notice things that were previously hidden in plain sight and also that help arrives from out of the blue, as you come to the place to take that great leap of faith and express exactly what you mean in a way beyond words.

Space between the Loops
On Socks and Mittens

In the Russian folktale, "The Mitten," a little boy's grandmother knits a beautiful pair of mittens for him. He loses one in the woods as he gathers wood for the fire. It lies on the woodland floor and becomes a resting place for all the animals in the forest. One by one, from the tiny mouse to the great bear, they squeeze into the cozy warm, wooly space. As the mitten in this story seems to miraculously contain all the animals of the woods, the mittens that we make contain the whole knitting universe. Ribbings and bind-offs for thumbholes, knit-togethers and pickups, increase for the hand, decrease for the top and tops of thumbs—if you can knit a mitten, you can knit anything. The techniques used in the mitten are the same ones needed to complete a larger garment. You can knit them in the round (my preferred method) or knit them flat and sew them up. They offer a little room to try out patterns and experiment with your own creativity. They are an advantageous tool for teaching a newcomer to knitting. All the important methods are quickly encountered, with the added benefit of a satisfying result.

To knit a pair of mittens is to warm two pairs of hands, much like the old adage that cutting wood warms you twice. Cold hands sinking into the warmth and care of wool in the wintertime is an experience to be coveted. Childhood snow days on the sledding hill and the idiot cord attached to your mitts and running through your sleeves, so as not to lose one; drying your wet hats, scarves, mittens, snowsuit, socks, and boots near the heat duct; cocoa and red runny noses—these memories fly back now, as you slip your hands into their warmth.

Mittens have cultural ties. The way a top is finished off and the way a cuff is knitted can show the culture from which it came. Is it from Scandinavia or Nova Scotia? Is the thumb gusseted on the side or placed on the palm?

The "northern" peoples of the world have embraced the lure and lore of the mitten. Duh, they needed them. Lizbeth Upitis in her book *Latvian Mittens* describes the importance, both of the mitten itself and of the significant patterns for them, to the Latvian people. The marriage culture of Latvia required the young women to prove their worth by the quality and quantity of their mittens and socks. In the past, these patterns were statements of identity—the unspoken sign that the wearer was a Latvian. Thanks to Upitis, you don't have to be Latvian to sport these treasures! And what about socks? Are they not mittens for the feet? What child hasn't put socks on his hands and called them "glubs"? Socks have the added technique of short rows at the heel, another stepping-stone along the path of knitting knowledge. Socks belie culture, too: Scottish kilt hose, Turkish stockings, the turn of the heel, the shape of the toe are all clues. They can be delicate or rough, for babies or for hunters, refined or sturdy. The styles and techniques are many and growing! Knitting, in general, is not a stagnant pond but a raging river. In my beginning days as a knitter, I remember thinking that if I could ever learn to make socks I would have "arrived." The knitting of socks seemed to me at that time the end-all evidence that I was indeed a master knitter! Of course, to discover the simplicity of socks is the paradox of knitting mastery. The simple is not necessarily remedial or basic, and the complicated is not necessarily mastery. I am always happy when I make socks.

But let's return to our story. We left all of the woodland animals snuggled together inside the warmth of the woolen mitten. At last, a cricket wanders over to the burgeoning mitten and asks to join the warmth. "No room, no room!" the others cry. "Certainly there's room for one more, a small one more such as myself?" and the cricket squeezes in, causing the mitten to burst, scattering all the inhabitants and leaving nothing but a small bit of red yarn hanging from a tree branch. Is there a lesson here? There is a point of overload for each of us and we need to be aware of what is too much. May you always have a sock or mitten on the needles!

Ethnic Knitting: Stories of Peoples

The myth that family patterns in Aran sweaters have been used for centuries to identify drowned sailors has been widely accepted, even by the Irish, and perpetuated by reputable sources including our favorite knitting sages. Richard Rutt sets the knitting world straight on the surface facts in *A History of Hand Knitting,* but he points to a deeper truth in the myth.

Life has always been a struggle on the windswept and stony Aran Islands, a twelve-mile boat trip from Ireland's shore. Running water wasn't brought there until the 1960s; telephones and electricity not until the 1970s. Despite the struggle of daily life, mothers began knitting sweaters with richly textured stitch patterns from home-spun, undyed wool (called *bainin,* pronounced baw-NEEN, meaning "whitish") for their sons' First Holy Communion in the 1920s and 1930s. Before then, no sweaters of any kind were worn on the Aran Islands. *The Aran Sweater* by Deirdre McQuillan reports, "One old man in his 80s, still fondly remembers his white First Communion gansey.... The imaginative leap from making stockings with some detail to larger items in which all sorts of patterns could be arranged had to do with a confident and shared experimentation.... Once experienced knitters could see the possibilities of patterning with no conventional forms to copy, there was no holding them back."[2]

The Aran sweaters were first sold in 1935 when Dr. Muriel Gahan, a supporter of Irish folk crafts, brought them to her store, the Country Shop in Dublin. The next year they were discovered by a textile journalist, Heinz Edgar Kiewe, who recognized their unique beauty and originality but saw a connection with early Celtic knot images. Sweater marketers picked right up on this, and before long Aran knitting was credited with thousands of years of history. A story from J. M. Synge's play *Riders to the Sea,* where the sister of a drowned man recognizes him by a dropped stitch in his sock, which she evidently had knit, was mixed up and mixed in with the Aran lore. But as Rutt says, "Kiewe's perception of the ethnic quality of Aran knitting, matched by the popular acceptance of its uniqueness, is not to be underrated. In a short time in a small community (about 2,500 in 1910 and 2,000 in 1936), Aran knitting evolved to express a singular communal feeling for design. The folk art of a community does not lack authenticity simply because it has a short history.... The patterns have a rough male Celtic beauty that needs no romanticizing, created by female skills. The women drew on levels of imagination that are earthier and more primitive than pseudo-religious allegories about the shapes of their patterns."[3] In other words, these women tapped into a source of connection not bound by time, and their expression enabled them to keep hearth and home together.

Other ethnic knitting, which survived in remote, rural areas around the world—including Nordic knitting, Icelandic yoke sweaters, socks from Eastern Europe and the Middle East, Fair Isle knitting, Shetland lace, Sanquhar gloves, Russian Orenburg lace shawls, English seaman ganseys, Bohus yokes, Andean caps, Scandinavian mittens, Faroe Island shawls, and Cowichan sweaters—enlarges and enriches the knitting culture with the nourishment of aesthetic achievements and possibilities.

There have been so many inspiring books that perpetuate the stories of these knitting cultures. (See the Resources section at the end of this book.) One that's back in print, and I refer to often myself, is Vibeke Lind's *Knitting in the Nordic Tradition,* first published in 1981 in Danish, and then in English translation in 1984. Lind included a comprehensive array of garments, in her words, "characteristic of Nordic knitting principles and pattern forms, based on practical and aesthetic values. The purpose of the book is not to give the reader the patterns themselves, but rather to suggest how one can use the models, changing them according to individual needs and the dictates of fashion. They should be an inspiration ... springboards for further development. Fixed points [that] can also serve to relieve the mind. Playing with form and material in this way, it is possible to renew oneself and to sharpen one's intellect."[4] Amen.

Space between the Loops
It All Starts Somewhere

From childhood, I have always sought out creative things, both to do and to look at. Both of my grandmothers were rural farmwives in Illinois, and quilting was their chosen pastime (or perhaps necessity). My mother is a skilled seamstress and crochets like a machine. As a child I learned these skills from my mother. I also played the guitar and enjoyed artistic endeavors. I grew up in Florida in a home where crafting and do-it-yourself-ism abounded. I learned sewing, embroidery, and crocheting as a child, but no one really knitted. Mother did make those popular garter stitch slippers one year for me and four siblings, and she taught me the long tail cast-on, but that was the end of her knitting career. When I was a young teenager, a neighbor taught me how to work a garter stitch, and I made several icky gold-colored items for an unknown baby. But I always felt that my garter stitch was strictly telling of my beginner-ness and was not enough to keep me interested. When I was about fifteen years old, my cousin came to live with us. She brought with her a small child's sweater that she was knitting. It was dark navy blue with light blue Norwegian Stars knitted into the body. I was intrigued, but not enough to knit myself.

Since Mom and I crocheted, we sought out places to buy yarn but mostly ended up at Kresge's (known later as K-Mart), purchasing Wintuk Orlon and Sayelle yarn for everything we made. And then there was the yarn shop that I mentioned in chapter 3, always in disarray with yarn everywhere in boxes and plastic bags. It was dingy and dusty and stale inside, but it was a place to get the different yarn and tools that could not be found in K-Mart. It was the kind of place that entered my imagination, rattling around until I found knitting. Color and texture jumbled everywhere like artist's paint on a palette halfway through the painting.

Time travel through marriage, a move to New York, and a two-year-old son. His naptime was my time to have tea and vegetate in front of public television. There she was, a charming English woman, showing off a Bohus sweater and talking about knitting like a fisherman baiting her hook. I was caught hook, line, and sinker. That woman was Elizabeth Zimmermann. My discovery of her was the beginning of my knitting life.

There was no one I knew who knitted. How to learn? I searched for a book or a magazine to begin, and learn I did. I do think that my basic skills in sewing and crocheting made it very easy for me to understand patterns. And when I didn't understand, I just said, "Oh well, I'll do it this way and hope it works out." I've always been sort of brave that way, but also felt like I was doing something wrong, not being able to figure out someone else's instructions. Hurray for Elizabeth Zimmermann, who gave permission and affirmation that I, indeed, was doing it right—for me.

Wisdom to Carry On

Before Elizabeth Zimmermann spread the word, American knitters suffered from a Victorian legacy in which, Priscilla A. Gibson-Roberts recounts in *Knitting in the Old Way,* knitting "became elevated to a feminine parlor art.... This ushered in the era of written instructions for elegant young ladies who didn't have the benefit of passed-down samplers and charts which had served the common folk so well for so long. Fashion garments, rather than the craft itself, became the focal point."[5] At Patternworks we were always delighted to encounter knitters who didn't depend on a pattern (although they usually came from other cultures).

Elizabeth Zimmermann (EZ, as devoted admirers call their wise "knitting mother") lovingly showed us the way to find our own way through knitting—and continues to do so through her videos and books. An artist, EZ was genuinely passionate about knitting and generously took us through her own creative process so we could get the idea of how to navigate the Knitting Way ourselves. Her books, *Knitting Without Tears* (which has saved many tears and started knitting careers), *Knitter's Almanac: Projects for Each Month of the Year, Knitting Workshop,* and *Knitting Around,* are such a good read because they're honest and funny and wise—full of spirit and energy we can use to light our own knitting candles. Elizabeth's videos with her daughter, Meg Swansen (who perpetuates the wisdom and the culture), were my first exposure to knitting as an intellectual romp. What an eye-opener! What fun! Writing this reminds me that I'm due for a video infusion. Maybe *The Knitting Glossary* this time.

And EZ was opinionated, a fact that she freely shared with her characteristic charm and good humor. One of her early professional knitting assignments was to write the pattern for an Aran sweater for *Vogue Knitting,* which was published in 1957. She was told to write the instructions using two-needle knitting, with a separate front, back, and sleeves, and to write them out, line by line, in words, rather than charts. I believe EZ's comment on the sense and clarity of these published instructions was something like "*#!?*."

EZ stood on her soapbox throughout her career, advocating the joys of circular knitting (the intuitive method used in folk or ethnic knitting styles) to avoid seams, to avoid purling (EZ's pet peeve), and in order to always view the right side as you work, a great advantage when knitting complicated pattern stitches as are used in Arans. She tried to free us from slavery to a printed pattern: (1) by showing us how to draw a sweater diagram as a visual plan to be marked with the number of stitches and inches you need to knit a sweater to your own specifications; (2) by using Elizabeth's Percentage System (EPS), which identifies a sweater's basic proportions that guide you to the numbers for your diagram; and (3) by charting stitch patterns, another visual aid. Priscilla A. Gibson-Roberts used EPS to create all the folk-sweater plans for *Knitting in the Old Way,* compiled so "today's knitter can once again be in control of the craft, knitting in the old way." Janice uses the outline plans for these sweaters as frames, to give her creative process a space to play.

As much as Elizabeth Zimmermann encouraged people not to be "blind followers" of written patterns, her legacy has been widely disseminated through her innovative projects. A few favorites are the Baby Surprise (a one-piece puzzle that, incredibly, folds into a great baby sweater), the Pi and the Pi Are Square Shawls, the Rib Warmer, and the Moccasin Sock.

"Writing things down is, I think, going to be important for me," she wrote in *Knitting Around.* "There are things that I remember, and things that I remember people telling me they remember, which will be gone for good when I finally die. This seems to me very sad. I wish I knew more about the people who went before me." Elizabeth wrote of connection in the service of finding one's own way in the world of knitting. It's a loving legacy.

My Story
I learned to knit from my paternal, "ethnic" grandmother who had emigrated from Russia. From exactly where I do not know, because family history was never discussed—on

either side. My lessons took place during a few short visits to her apartment when I was eight or nine. I remember the long, tortuous strand that formed on the first row after casting on, using the e-wrap cast-on method Grandma taught me, which was a common method at the time. It wasn't until years later, when I first knit in the round and tried to figure out why my stitches twisted, that I noticed everyone else didn't knit into the back of the stitch. Later, at Patternworks, I discovered that this was an Eastern European style of knitting. There was no love lost between the two sides of my family. When my temper flared or I committed some other transgression, my mother and my "American-born" maternal grandmother placed my origin on "the other side." I didn't feel accepted by my knitting grandmother, either (who, I felt, considered me on the other "other side"). She was not pleased with my work and suggested that I concentrate on what I was doing, and not watch TV when I knit—advice I didn't follow. Although my mother and her mother (who spent a great deal of time in our apartment) knew how to knit and crochet, I don't believe I ever saw either of them working on a craft of any kind during my childhood.

During high school I remember knitting a gray seed-stitch jacket for my mother and sewing a dress for her with the sewing machine I received as my choice over the alternate option of a Sweet Sixteen party. As a teen, I heard the message that I had "golden hands" modified by "all you need is a rocking chair and a cat." The next thing I recall knitting was a sweater for my fiancé. On the walk home from Brooklyn College, I went to the cut-rate yarn store and selected Germantown wool. I believe it was a classic white, cabled, V-neck tennis sweater with red and blue stripes around the neck, sleeves, and bottom. I can actually picture myself sitting in my mother's dark living room, happily knitting and, you've got it, watching TV, although I can't remember the finished product. Considering that white smooth yarn showcases every stitch, and set-in sleeves and V-necks need to be finished with finesse, forgetting in this case is probably a blessing. It's strange how much I've forgotten about my early knitting. However, I can recall the rush of pleasure I felt when I brought home that bag of yarn. It's as intense today with each new project.

I never took advantage of the bustling full-service yarn store a few blocks from where I lived, although I must have set foot in there because I can picture the warm, yarn-rich atmosphere, where hanks were wound into balls for customers who sat at a table knitting, and instruction was given. It was a golden opportunity for initiation into the knitting culture. I was blind to it at the time. Instead I went it alone, using my knitting as an escape. I wasn't much of a reader at the time, but I picked up basic skills in my own idiosyncratic ways, here and there. Still, it was through knitting that Patternworks was conceived, and that's where I began to find openings to worlds I had not known.

Seeking the River of Connection

Janice and I went to a wonderful fiftieth birthday party one Saturday night that set me to thinking. These days, as I've said, I'm finding connections everywhere. The friends and relatives gathered to help celebrate were all openly and copiously affectionate, and the music and dancing was straight from and to the heart, no holding back. Sharyn Faranda is a person connected to those around her. She was surrounded by family and friends of great diversity and was at ease with everyone. I was moved to move with the live music (performed by a fabulous band led by her husband, Kenny, who brings to music what Sharyn brings to knitting), but I wasn't dancing as the celebrants were all around me. That's right: I'm still not dancing. I might add that Janice wasn't either. I brought that up at our next meeting. Note: Janice reported that she was dancing on the inside, imagining her fingers on the strings of the guitar, and she didn't need to prove that. Besides, she says, she was totally connected to the musicians on the stage, immersed in the sound of the dance. Music is another mathematical language with patterns and meaning that speaks to the spirit.

Sharyn rises every morning around dawn and knits. It's the way she centers herself for the day, as other people might meditate or pray. Her knitting is organic and alive as bread rising in the kitchen. Her Debbie Bliss bunnies had more than personality. They were animated and real and wanted to be your friend.

But, alas, Sharyn told a sad story at the party. She was showing us the beautiful shawl a friend had knit her as a gift, and I blurted out, "That's like bringing coals to Newcastle!" That's when she told us that she had looked forward to a hand-knit blanket from her grandmother when her first child (and her grandmother's first great-grandchild) was born, because it was her tradition to knit a wonderful baby blanket for each of her fifty-two grandchildren. No blanket came and Grandma said, "Oh, I would never knit for you." That hurts. Isn't it true that there's no one who appreciates the value of a hand-knit gift more than a knitter?

Somehow, the party started me thinking about the difference between *culture* and *cultured*. Mary Thomas's wonderful books that clearly show and transmit a passion for the craft also show a "cultured," tailored style of knitting. Mary Thomas refers to the style of knitting that Elizabeth Zimmermann introduced us to—what I consider intuitive and freeing—as "peasant" (a term that could be used before euphemisms were politically correct), because it was a product of ethnic subcultures.

June Hemmons Hiatt in her comprehensive and controversial three-pound volume *Principles of Knitting: Methods and Techniques of Hand Knitting* (referred to as POK, currently out of print—and the lone knitting book among "the top 10 most sought-after US out of print books of 2004" at BookFinder.com—but in the process of revision) stands in the cultured/tailored camp, with Mary Thomas. I took a class with Hiatt once and was dazzled by her skills and understanding of fit (she analyzed why the raglan cardigan I was wearing dragged to the back and, to my befuddlement, prescribed darts at the lower front) and enjoyed her generous teaching style, but I no more wanted to live up to that level of tailored knitting than I wanted to lift a house. My solution was to give away the sweater and never knit myself another raglan, since they don't work "as is" for my body type.

POK, in Hiatt's words, "is an affectionate but critical look at this fine old craft.... Even the most advanced knitter will have a legacy of methods that may not really be the best in a given situation. I have gone back to the beginning and have questioned, examined, and tested even the most fundamental aspects of knitting [and she's not kidding], trying to look at each with new eyes. I wanted to know why a technique behaved the way it did, under what circumstances it worked best, and whether or not it could be improved or there was an alternate method that worked better.... There are countless regional variations and little oddments of knowledge that are not generally known. I have sought out and tested any obscure technique that I could find, rejecting some and delighting in others that I hope will find wider use.... Just as I did, I think you may find some of your most cherished and dependable techniques called into question." Hiatt presents eight pages of pros and cons on knitting sweaters in the round and concludes, "All in all, it seems to me that knitting in the round brings with it certain risks and quite a few compromises, and unless the garment is one that would be particularly enhanced by being seamless, it should be avoided."[6] This really hit a nerve in the seamless camp. Some knitters responded with anger. Flames burned through the Internet. How can the wound be healed?

We knitters are passionate about our craft, our work,

our methods. Hiatt is a clinician, analytical and precise. She has a point of view and makes valid points that may come across as dogmatic. The seamless camp's point of view is just as valid. Listening to someone we don't agree with is a good thing. That's what makes the knitting world expansive and inclusive. EZ wrote, in *Knitting Without Tears,* "There is no right way to knit; there is no wrong way to knit. The way to knit is the way that suits you, and the way that suits the wool and the pattern and the shape that you are currently working on.... So if anybody kindly tells you that what you are doing is 'wrong,' don't take umbrage; they mean well. Smile submissively, and listen, keeping your disagreement on an entirely mental level. They may be right, in this particular case, and even if not, they may drop off pieces of information which will come in very handy if you file them away carefully in your brain for future reference."[7] Knitting is *your* experience. Your experience belongs to you. Knit as though you have nothing to prove.

I once took a knitting class, at one of the early national knitting conventions in the 1980s, with a woman teaching an intarsia technique using a device she had patented. About halfway through the class, after my yarns tangled over and over, I realized that this wasn't for me and excused myself. I believe the instructor commented: "We can't all be classy knitters." It's true that I abhor intarsia knitting—typically assisted by the use of bobbins wound with the different color yarns hanging from the back—probably for the same reason I don't like painting. I have a hard time keeping the materials from running amok. For color work, I much prefer Fair Isle knitting, which uses only two colors in a row and establishes a rhythm. It is most agreeably, in my opinion, knitted in the round, so you always face the right side. Intarsia can't be knit in the round without innovative contortions. Why did I take the class? I was probably still looking for a magic bullet.

As an aside, Kaffe Fassett freed intarsia from bobbins when he switched his medium from paint to yarn after happening upon a woman knitting on a train. His sweaters were complicated yarn paintings in *glorious color* (the title of one of his books), using dozens of colors in short-enough lengths to dispense with bobbins. It was an innovative and freer process in which a strand could be more easily extracted from the tangle. Fassett also advocated knitting ends in as you go. The sweaters took the knitting world by storm in the 1980s. I was never drawn in enough to try my hand at one, partly because the knitting was still unrhythmic, a perfectly valid option (but not for me—unless, at times, to delight a grandchild), but partly because of "reverse snobbery." I felt they were too "rich for my blood" at the time when high-end Kaffe Fassett kits by Rowan were popular: an unexamined tug from my peasant roots whence the knitting came? It's remarkable how much we can see of our deepest selves in our projects.

Back to healing the wound. Perhaps Bashō, the Zen poet, pointed to a remedy: "Do not seek to follow in the footsteps of the wise; seek what they sought." To follow in the footsteps of the wise one, who found her own knitting way and encouraged us to find our own, read what she had to say.

"Once upon a time there was an old woman who loved to knit. She lived with her Old Man in the middle of a woods in a curious one-room schoolhouse which was rather untidy, and full of wool. Every so often as she sat knitting by the warm iron stove or under the dappled shade of the black birch, as the season might dictate, she would call out to her husband: 'Darling, I have unvented something,' and would then go on to fill his patient ears with enthusiastic but highly unintelligible and esoteric gabble about knitting. At last one day he said, 'Darling, you ought to write a book.' 'Old man,' she said, 'I think I will.' So she did," wrote Elizabeth Zimmermann, on the opening page of her *Knitter's Almanac.*[8]

Yarn Worlds Not Altogether Possible

Strangely enough, it was in the commercial world of marketing yarn that I first encountered art in the spiritual way that American poet W. S. Merwin described: "Art itself is not altogether possible (it is one of the things about it that we prize), and yet it exists, for all that—just as we live not only in the absolute but at the same time in the world of the necessary and the possible."[9] I had the good fortune of being forced to enter the "not altogether possible" worlds of color and design that were made possible by two different artists, Kristin Nicholas and Maie Landra. Each of these women created a real-world fairy-tale kingdom of color and design that sprang from a strong internal vision. Each seems incredibly complex to the outsider, yet is in complete harmony within—which is why all its many magical colors work together—and has attracted a huge following of knitters who share an understanding with the others inside its loop.

One of these artists, Kristin Nicholas, reveals the key in Melanie D. Falick's 1996 celebration of knitters, *Knitting in America*. "I understand the concept of the white room and sparseness, Scandinavian and modern design," Kristin says, "but I can't live there." The distinctive world of color and design created in Kristin's sixteen years as creative director at Classic Elite Yarns, and now as a freelance designer, in her home decoration, pottery, paintings, and book illustrations, emerges from a clear internal vision that seamlessly translates into everything she does. This inner/outer harmony allows Kristin to be incredibly prolific, since every action seems to naturally flow out of her core. She wrote in an e-mail, "To me all of the things we do—knitting, sewing, gardening, painting, cooking ... have a spiritual side." Visit www.KristinNicholas.com for a glimpse of Kristin's work, which, she says, "is especially inspired by ethnic textiles. Favorite sources ... are Indian saris and embroideries, Turkish and Persian carpets, Peruvian knitwear, and embroideries from the Bukhara region of China." The utter harmony in the midst of such complexity creates a remarkable oasis of comfort and inspiration.

Kristin's home was shown in the August 2004 issue of *Country Home* and featured on the cover. Looking for the article, you know you've found it when the color goes from Kansas to Oz. "Once I started decorating houses," she says, "I realized that it's only paint and time. So, if it doesn't work, just repaint it." About knitting, which she came back to as a college student with the help of *Knitting Without Tears* and a stitch treasury, Kristin says she does most of her designing "on the needles" and makes notes on graph paper as she knits. In an e-mail, she writes, "Personally, I love to chop onions and garlic before cooking them at suppertime. It gives me time to wind down. I guess it is the same feeling that lots of knitters have just sitting and knitting. For me, when I am knitting I am thinking about the next design—so it isn't very relaxing." Perhaps that's explained by Kristin's comment, quoted in *Knitting in America:* "In America, the school system teaches you to follow rules, but you've got to know when to break them, how to change things, to make them better, to make them suit you."[10] A spiritual experience can be described as enlivening rather than relaxing. It's a brave thing to step outside your comfort zone, break a rule, change something, but to get to that spiritual place takes a hero's journey down to the deep places in your soul.

When we started printing parts of the Patternworks catalog in color, I wanted to sell Classic Elite yarns, but I felt as though I was coming into the middle of a story. The culture and mystique had been evolving for a decade and so much was unwritten and there were so many colors. It was a luscious environment, but it seemed you had to be initiated into it by word of mouth. I couldn't find the kind of linear order I understood. I started with Kristin's ethnically inspired World Knit Collection Kits (Ferociously Fun Sock, Tea Cozies, Bags, Vests, Inspired Interiors, and Eccentric Gifts), which were easy to understand, but challenging to knit. The kit included a basket packed with several skeins of yarn in different colors and basic patterns with charts to create your own designs. The color photo included in the kit showed glorious examples (which were created by a knitting guild from the kits). However, there were no instructions to knit specifically what was in the photo. You had to figure it out yourself. In a culture where knitters depend on patterns, this should have been a merchandising disaster. But something that seemed not altogether possible happened, and they were a huge success, with nary a kit returned.

To get an idea of the yarn phenomenon created by the mother/daughter team of Maie and Taiu Landra—the combined genius and vision of Maie's art and Taiu's business acumen—try doing an Internet search for "Koigu addiction." Koigu was the name of a family farm in Estonia, the country of Maie's birth. Their first yarn, KPPPM (Koigu Painter's Palette Premium Merino, and KPM solids)—spun to Maie's specifications, each skein a hand-painted work of art—was one of the best selling and least returned yarns at Patternworks, defying rational understanding.

When Maie and Taiu exhibited the yarn next to us at one of the Knitting Guild of America regional markets, I ignored it. I thought it was too lightweight to be popular (knitting at 7 or 8 stitches to an inch). But René Katz, who was helping me out, couldn't keep from fingering it through the slats of their display crates. We struck up a conversation. Then came the struggle, over time, to get me to understand their world of color and design, and to figure out how to sell it in a catalog. The colors had no names, just numbers: three digits for KPPPM and four digits for KPM solids. Weren't color names essential to convey an image to the knitter? Now knitters are comfortable communicating through numbers, such as P413, which signify realities beyond words. Another problem that rational thinking threw in my path was that the colors were one of a kind, and there were *lots* of them, painted like Maie's watercolors—so new dye lots were new representations of the color. Another roadblock to selling this world of color through a catalog was that color printing is far from accurate—compounding the problem of the non-repeatable dye lot shown in the photo. Does selling this yarn in a catalog sound possible? Add to that the fact that Maie's patterns are the work of a genius, using many colors in ways not easily translated by another knitter. There was even a support group on the Internet for at least one design, the legendary Oriental Jacket.

But the validity of these seemingly solid, rational arguments dissipated like smoke as the reality of the Koigu world emerged. It was a success from the start. How could it be that there were virtually no complaints when customers received colors that were completely different than those pictured? It's not the way things work in the conventional world of yarn. At first we fretted when our Koigu shipments arrived, but gradually we relaxed into the flow of an alternate reality.

Customers and staff alike stood reverently and paid homage before the Koigu palette on the shelves in a glowing example of Janice's reminder, "It is what it is." And what it is *is* art. When we accept the mystery, we find ourselves in a state of grace.

Using Knitting to Tell a Story

Artists who use knitting as their medium express their inner stories through their art, as all artists do.

A show at Long Island University's Salena Gallery in 2003, titled *Meditation for the Hand Artworks,* "developed through meditative absorption and through the repetitious movements of the brush, pencil [or needles] ... a kind of chanting with the hand," which included two hundred feet of knitting by a Norwegian knitting commune in Oslo that formed a spiral on the gallery floor.

The Chicago Museum of Contemporary Art in 2001 exhibited *Knitting for My Soul,* performance art by Paté

Conaway, in which the artist sat in the gallery and knit each day, creating a pair of mittens large enough to cover his body, at a gauge of 8 stitches equals 1 foot, with 4-foot needles, and white cotton piping "yarn" wound in 5-foot diameter balls. Conaway says he began knitting when working with senior citizens as an artist in residence and became frustrated when they weren't interested in the art projects he tried to introduce. He "gave up" and let one of the women teach him to knit a washcloth. After finding a needle "about the size of a turkey baster" in a drawer, he got involved with what they *were* interested in—on a big scale. "I would be working in the hobby shop of the retirement home [on a washcloth the size of a queen-sized bed], and the knitting was like a magnet; it pulled people in … a dialogue began. I was asked many times, 'Why are you doing this?' That is a wonderful challenge, because I have to stand behind it as an artist and think, 'Why *am* I doing this? What is this all about?' And I was able to say, 'It's modern art; it's sculpture.' So we've made a complete circle—I've taken their language of knitting, translated into *my* language by shifting the scale, and now we have modern art, a sculpture." About the monthlong performance, Conaway says his sculptor side would have preferred knitting the mittens in his studio and displaying the finished product, and was annoyed about entering the gallery space with just his needles and a giant ball of yarn: "I realized that part of being an artist for me is not only to share my art, but also to share my process."

Moving from performance art, we read an online article at www.knitjapan.co.uk/exhib.htm about a group of "ordinary Japanese women and housewives with common enthusiasm for knitting" who became part of a workshop geared to make them "look at their hobby from the point of view of professionals or artists," according to Yoshimi Kihara, the knitting designer who led the group called Fushiginoiroito Workshop (puzzling, strange, mysterious colored yarns). Kihara said, "It was my belief that we should show ourselves to the public in our exhibitions without covering up all the struggle involved for better or worse. Sometimes time and patience would run out before we had finished, but nevertheless we would carry on with the exhibition, even if it was half-finished."

Group member Kazumi Saeki added, "Another theme that I have been struggling with for many years is the plain surface.... Knitted surfaces have an appearance that is made by the existence of each stitch, and because this structure traps the light inside it I feel as if the colors appear from the inside of each stitch." These artists have come to terms with the acceptance and expression of that which lies within. Knitting, for them, is beyond knitting a hat or a sweater. It's about reaching their souls.

Knitting Stories in the News

"To arrive without my knitting in Peru where so many women are at it is like arriving naked at a knitting convention," begins Susie Emmett's 2002 report for the BBC News. "Shy and understandably suspicious of my questions about their lives ... it was my genuine appreciation of the skills at these fingertips that breaks the nervous tension between us." One fifty-seven-year-old woman, Anatolia, says she knits twelve hours a day because she needs the money. Does she find it a burden? Anatolia answers, "I set all my troubles aside. I escape from them when I knit. That's the secret." Some women do have to knit in secret to keep the extra income from their husbands who would withhold money for household expenses if they knew. Some lie about where they're going when they steal away for a few hours of knitting in a "safe house." "My husband tells me I pay more attention to my knitting than either him or our children. But the only work he has is washing cars in the street. He can be days without money. My knitting gives us everything we have." Sitting with three generations of women as they knitted on a riverbank, Emmett observes, "After days of research and interviews, this time

I felt no need to ask more questions. It was enough to sit in silence together, sharing what we had in common."

A reporter for the *Philadelphia Inquirer*, Natalie Pompilio, writes the story of a young woman who knits to build community. "For the founder of a 'radical' group, needlework and social change are bound together. Shjra EtShalom [who is also an activist in Radical Menstruation] is rarely without her knitting needles or her sense of justice. Only 19, she's an accomplished knitter with countless scarves, sweaters and blankets to her credit. She's also fiercely antiwar, pro–workers' rights and fervent about making a positive difference in the world.... EtShalom formed 'Sew What?! Radical Knitters' in September [2003]. About thirty members—ranging in age from six to fifty but with a core of twenty-somethings—meet bi-weekly ... 'Sitting in a circle of people and knitting and chatting and asking questions ... is a very sweet way to build a community,' EtShalom said ... 'I was always known as the little knitting girl.'... Now she's the knitting woman, and she's happy with that."

"Radical Knitting: Knitting Is Hot" by Vanessa Richmond in the *Tyee* online journal focuses on another feisty group of knitters. "'Radical domestic culture' is how members of one Stitch 'n' Bitch group in Dunbar [British Columbia] jokingly describe their passion. They aim to launch a tongue-in-cheek public art piece that involves knitted sweaters for outdoor sculptures. Member Rachel Poliquin, twenty-nine, a PhD student in Comparative Literature at UBC [University of British Columbia], even has a plan to knit 'knickers for the bull's bits' on the bovine sculpture that stands outside the brokerage office at Georgia and Homer. 'Public sculptures are often so sensible and so male,' says Poliquin. 'Wouldn't it be great if one morning they were all just covered in knitting?' There's even talk of knitting scarves for skyscrapers."

During the time when women were arrested for being "improperly veiled" and poor children were sent to war "armed only with gold-painted 'keys to heaven,'" Marjane Satrapi writes in *Persepolis,* her story of coming of age in Iran during revolution and war, "I got to go to my first party. Not only did my mom let me go, she also knitted me a sweater full of holes and made me a necklace with chains and nails. Punk rock was in."

Life Stories

For these women knitting was important in their lives, serving as a guide for themselves and providing a profound way to reach out to others.

A touching obituary in the *Boston Globe* for Marjorie MacDonald reads: "The mother of eight, Mrs. MacDonald acted as the neighborhood mother as well.... There were always plenty of 'kids and cats' running around the house, her daughter Elaine Farrell of Brockton said, but 'my mother was very calm and cool and she just went with the flow.... Once when [Farrell] was planning on going ice skating with a friend who lost a glove, her mother told her to hold on for 20 minutes and 'she just sat there and whipped up another mitten.'"

Juana (Angelica) Larnia Estratta was remembered in the *San Antonio Express News:* "To her daughter's teaching companions and to kindergarten students, she was 'Abuelita Angelica,' the kind Peruvian lady who made them wool slippers known as 'botines,' or booties." When she came to live in San Antonio, Texas, Angelica "brought with her a fondness for knitting, a craft she had learned only a few years earlier while visiting sisters in Rochester, New York. 'It was almost like I was born to make these botines. I got better and better and started mixing colors, and I added the pompom on top that people really like.'" At www.Novica.com, a website founded by her grandsons, Angelica wrote a poignant autobiography. In recent years, she said, "I've made thousands of botines. Thousands! I've sent them to Spain, Australia, Peru, New York all over. I've made them for the Methodist churches.

I've given them to the elderly at a retirement home to keep their feet from getting cold. I even sent them to Brazil for the family as a gift when my grandson was married there.... Once in Spain, a millionaire woman asked me to make her a pair in white; White?! Why white, I thought. They would get dirty. But I made them and ... the woman loved them. She wrote me and told me that she uses her botines every day. Even to sleep!" The obituary in the *Express News* goes on to say, "In 1999, Larnia began dialysis and soon started knitting booties for staff and other patients. The great-grandmother ceased production two years ago when arthritis made it difficult for her to use knitting needles."

The *New York Times* eulogized another knitter: "Helen Bunce died on February 24 at a nursing home in Watertown, NY, where she was known as the Mitten Lady. She was eighty-six and had been knitting mittens until a few days before her death. Mrs. Bunce had been a legend in Watertown and in international church circles for decades, although until December only a few people knew she was the Mitten Lady whose anonymous handmade donations to an annual church clothing drive spread her fame far and wide.... 'She could knit in her sleep,' her daughter Helen MacDonald, said yesterday, estimating that her mother had knitted at least four thousand pairs of mittens over the last forty-seven years, and perhaps a lot more.... For all the mittens she turned out, the Mitten Lady sobriquet was somewhat misleading. Mrs. Bunce, who knew that little heads as well as hands needed protection against the cold, knitted a matching cap for every pair of mittens. The sets included a handwritten tag saying, 'God Loves You, and So Do I....' Mrs. Bunce, who always made it a point to start a new pair of mittens or a cap as soon as one was completed (on the assumption, she once explained, that God would not let anything happen to her as long as she had unfinished work), apparently knew the end was near. When she died, her daughter said, her needles were empty. Mrs. Bunce's husband of 67 years, Karl [who shared a room at the nursing home with his beloved wife], died [three days later] February 27."

Eleanor Roosevelt was described by Adlai Stevenson as a person who "would rather light candles than curse the darkness—and her glow has warmed the world." Her knitting bag was publicly recognized as one of the important objects of the twentieth century, displayed in an exhibition called "Looking Back on the American Century" at the Harry S. Truman Presidential Library and Museum in 2000. Eleanor's grandson, John Roosevelt Boettiger, reminisced, "I was born in Seattle, Washington, on March 30, 1939, toward the end of my grandfather's second term as president, and as the world was about to go to hell. My grandmother Eleanor, who was in later years to become my most significant mentor, held her daughter's hand during the hardest part of my difficult delivery, and very likely sat quietly knitting during the rest." One time, when reporters chased Eleanor to find out where she was going, wrote Blanche Wiesen Cook in *Eleanor Roosevelt: The Defining Years, 1933–1938*, she stopped the car, reached for her knitting bag and told them calmly, "It's nice here in the shade, and I like to knit. I'm willing to sit here all day if I have to, but I'm not going to tell you where we're going."

Fred Rogers, host of the beloved children's public television show *Mr. Rogers' Neighborhood*, is connected in many people's memories with his knitted cardigans. The *New York Times* said in 2003, "When the Smithsonian Institution put one of Mr. Rogers's zippered sweaters on exhibit in 1984, no one who had grown up with American television would have needed an explanation. He had about two dozen of those cardigans. Many had been knitted by his mother. He wore one every day as part of the comforting ritual that opened the show: Mr. Rogers would come home to his living room—a set at WQED-TV in Pittsburgh—and change from a sports coat and loafers into sweater and sneakers as he sang the words of his theme, 'It's a beaut-i-ful day in the neighborhood ... won't you be my neighbor?'" Fred Rogers was an ordained minister and certainly knew about spiritual connection. He asked, "Have you had people who have touched you—not moved you in order to manipulate you—but touched you inside-to-inside? Take a minute to think of at least one person who helped you to become who you are inside today. Someone who was interested in you for who you really are, someone you feel really accepted the essence of your being. Just one minute, one minute to think of those who have made a real difference in your life."

Elsa Schiaparelli recognized and engaged in the dance of life, which she showed in her description of the creation of fashion as "born by small facts, trends, or even politics, never by trying to make little pleats and furbelows, by trinkets, by clothes easy to copy, or by the shortening or lengthening of a skirt." In other words, fashion is about recognizing the Spirit of the Times. A 1928 hand-knit trompe l'oeil sweater, with a knitted-in bow and collar and cuff detail that fooled the eye, "got Schiaparelli's career off to a fast start ... and introduced the notion that clothing could be a self-aware visual joke. It became a style sensation for several seasons in New York and London as well as Paris and was widely copied. She expanded to sportswear (including knit bathing suits with tattoo motifs)," according to an article by Roberta Smith in the *New York Times*. The story goes that, in Paris, she admired a friend's sweater, which she describes in her autobiography *Shocking Life* as "definitely ugly in color and shape." However, Schiaparelli recognized the unique qualities of the knitting style—which Richard Rutt described in *A History of Hand Knitting*—and hunted down the knitter, whom she referred to as "an Armenian peasant" and from whom she commissioned a black sweater with white knitted-in trim. After two unsuccessful attempts, she declared the third one "sensational." When the first order for forty sweaters came in, the knitter rounded up other knitters and found "some good cheap" yarn, which appears to be Shetland wool. The *Ladies Home Journal* even published knitting instructions during the craze. In conjunction with the 2003 exhibition, "Shocking! The Art and Fashion of Elsa Schiaparelli" at the Philadelphia Museum of Art, the museum began selling kits, including Shetland wool and the pattern, for $150 and offered the finished sweater for $850. Rutt points out that two yarns are used throughout (even in the solid black or white sections.) The yarn "not appearing at the front is woven in behind at every fourth stitch" and the stitches at which the weaving is done are staggered on alternate rows. This weaving gives a tweedy effect and produces a stable fabric that holds its shape. One of Schiaparelli's Twelve Commandments for Women is this: "Never shop with another woman, who sometimes consciously, and often unconsciously, is apt to be jealous." Now knitting with another woman—that's another story.

Anne Rubin, although not a knitter, appreciated and understood the connection between the past and the present through knitting. Rubin "had one surpassing passion in her life, and it was shopping," commented Lynn Hirschberg in her article in the *New York Times* on the life of someone who loved knits, rather than knitting, and traveled the world to find the best. "These are classics," Hirschberg said in the article, "as I lusted after yet another sweater, this one knit in a yellow-and-black pattern that resembled clamshells, Rubin reflected, 'These clothes look like now, but they were only possible then.... There aren't those ladies in the countryside anymore. And this is all that's left from them.... History comes in many *forms*. Sometimes you can wear it.'" Connection comes in many forms, too, and sometimes you can reach it through knitting. Oh, if we could spend some time with these sweaters and a tape measure.

Space between the Loops
Connecting the Generations

"My grandmother used to knit me skating costumes, winter sweaters with matching scarves and mittens. I was always outfitted in matching wool sets. She's eighty-seven now and spends the winter months, when the possibility of lawn bowling in Canada is limited, knitting memories for her granddaughters. This week an envelope arrived in my mail box full of tiny samples of yarn and a pattern for an afghan. I chose five colors and returned the envelope to her, aware of her presence in my own art making processes. Knitting needles pierce through skin memories; daughters-mothers-grandmothers longing to stitch themselves through time." So writes Stephanie Springgay in an article titled "Cloth as Intercorporality" in the *International Journal of Education and the Arts*.

Even the Yarn Tells a Story

A strand of yarn, a bit longer than three yards, tells a story of Norse explorations in the thirteenth century, according to an article by Päivi Suonmi at the All Fiberarts website. Fifteen years after the almost eight-hundred-year-old strand was found buried in the Arctic tundra, Patricia Sutherland, the associate curator of the Canadian Museum of Civilization, noticed that it was similar to fragments she had seen at an archaeological excavation of a medieval Norse farm. It was a blend of goat hair and fur from the Arctic hare. Inuit people, who did not spin, had inhabited Baffin Island, where the strand was found, from 500 BCE to the sixteenth century, suggesting "a visit to the region by a Norse ship." As a result of this insight about the strand, the museum is conducting an archaeology project that "could reveal additional information about the contacts between the Norse and the Aboriginal peoples of the eastern Arctic." Sutherland has since found additional evidence of spun yarn at other sites on Baffin Island. "Radiocarbon dating of the spun yarn samples indicates that a European presence may have begun earlier than previously thought." Such a big story in such a small strand of yarn.

An Attitude of Gratitude

David Rucker, who introduces some customs and traditions of knitting in a fanciful setting in his "Event at the River," one of seven stories in *Tales in Time: Volume Two*, written for seven- to twelve-year-olds, says, "The telling of stories at the close of day is tradition as old as language itself. It is a time for magical fantasy, and for the teaching of customs, traditions, and concepts." He leads the reader to ponder the gift of hands and connection in the following excerpt. "'It's lovely,' said the visitor. 'Where does one buy a sweater for a tube creature around these parts?' 'Snake, I'm a snake,' said Snake. 'Not a tube. Snakes must knit their own sweaters. Stores are only for humans such as yourself.' 'But you have no hands,' said the visitor.... 'You are indeed right,' replied Snake.... 'Snakes simply need a knitting partner.... Aunt Slither is my Mother's knitting partner.' ... 'I'll bet you can knit by yourself?' blurted Snake. 'Uhm, why yes,' responded the visitor. 'Although I had never thought about it as "by myself." Usually two or three of us knit together, I mean, at the same time. We have tea, and we visit. It's nice to be with one's friends.'"[11]

Experience It for Yourself

Write *your* knitting story. Open a dialog with yourself by asking and answering some questions, and not necessarily in this order:

What was my first knitting experience?

Who was my first knitting teacher?

What did my teacher, my mom, or my grandma think of my knitting?

How did that make me feel?

Do I have any knitting wounds?

How did I take off from there?

What are the colors of my projects?

Why do I choose certain colors or reject them?

Which times of my life are encapsulated in these projects?

In which projects did I express myself?

Where are the projects now?

What are my pet peeves?

What does knitting mean to me?

How important is it in my life now?

Do I connect with others through my knitting?

Is this connection positive and expansive?

When was the last time I tried something new?

Do I ever break out and break the rules?

Who do I knit with?

When do I knit?

How do I feel in a yarn shop?

How do I feel about my yarn stash?

How do I keep it?

Do I expect it to outlive me?

Do I have any knitting fantasies?

What are my knitting secrets?

Am I hiding yarn in the trunk of my car?

Do I need an addition to my home to house my yarn stash?

You are safe here with friends. We're all in the same knitting boat. We aren't going to write *The Yarn Store Diaries*. This is a place to honestly explore the stories of your life.

The Bearable Lightness of Knitting

Learning to Let Go of Perfection

Freedom from Perfection

During the writing of this book, I got a phone call to tell me that my son had had a stroke. I grabbed some different shades of multicolored yarn and a set of interchangeable needles and caught the first plane to Boca Raton. I started a shawl for chapter 9, "Paying It Forward." After knitting from the second ball of yarn for a while, I thought the colors didn't go well together at all. I started a different color. I was still unhappy with the way the colors looked, but I kept going. Thankfully Danny's condition rapidly improved, and eight days later on the plane home, on my fourth color way, I decided to start a stitch pattern: 3 knit, 3 purl for 3 rows; then break it up by continuing in garter stitch for a few rows, and back to 3 knit, 3 purl. I noticed that I had "messed up" on the second set of 3–3. Instead of ripping out, I decided to start changing from knit to purl and back again when the color changed in the strand, letting the yarn dictate a free-form pattern. Sometimes I let the strand dictate the change; other times the next stitch on the needle decided whether I'd knit or purl. I made up a rule that if the strand was the same color as the next stitch it would be a knit. It became an adventure! I went with whatever whim floated by. I started changing the stitch based on how the combination of the strand and the stitch struck me.

A graceful, undulating stitch pattern formed. "Wow," I thought. Then, for some reason, maybe one of my recent discussions with Janice on knitting whimsy, I felt compelled to unply and braid the yarn ends at the color changes and allow a curly fringe to unfurl past a securing knot. I think I like it! It's hard to explain how freeing that whole process felt. I began to think of the project as a comfort shawl for myself. I thought I would like to thread ribbon through the increase eyelets, as you would in a baby blanket. I was so excited about the idea that I stopped in a fabric store on the way home from the airport and picked up a narrow satin ribbon in a beautiful burgundy color that brought together the varied shades of the different color ways of the yarn (which happened to be Koigu's Kersti, named after Taiu's daughter). Heaven! (I'm looking forward to trying Julia, a yarn Kristin Nicholas designed and named after her own little girl.) This was one time I allowed myself to let go of "rules" and was rewarded with much more than comfort. I had lulled my critical voice into a peaceful rest and exulted in feeling alive! I haven't often (maybe never?) given myself that kind of break. I now highly recommend it to you.

I've come to find out that complicated natural systems, even the human heart, aren't perfectly regular. "Tiny fluctuations in cardiac rhythm are, in fact, a sign of the heart's health, a display of its robust condition. Physicians have even discovered that when they detect a heartbeat becoming increasingly mechanical and regular, it's a signal of problems, a sign the heart lacks flexibility. It's become brittle," according to *The Seven Life Lessons of Chaos*.[1]

Perfection means "complete," rather than without error. The truth of wisdom is that if you think you're there, you're not.

Space between the Loops
Some Advice—and a Warning—about Obsession in the Pursuit of Perfection

Move toward passionate, playful knitting that flows— activities that encourage living in the process, letting unbridled inspiration run away with the product and away from avid knitting that's driven and closed. The perfect yarn, the perfect pattern, the perfect garment become the pursuit. We find the perfect yarn, but it lies in our stash waiting for the perfect pattern. We find the perfect pattern but can't find the perfect yarn.

Perfection is pursued in our work, every stitch perfect, no missed increases or decreases, pattern followed perfectly, the result, a perfect work. There's a saying in Bluegrass music, "If it's too good, it ain't good."

In 1837 Honoré de Balzac wrote "The Unknown Masterpiece," a story set in seventeenth-century Paris, centered around an aging artist named Frenhofer, who is thought to be the greatest artist of his time. He arrives at the studio of a student who is entertaining another young artist. After a discourse on perfection of light and brush-stroke and the completion of a painting, Frenhofer reveals that he has been working for years on a secret painting that has consumed all of his creative powers, but he needs a model of perfect beauty to finish his work. Curious, the young artists procure a young woman to model for Frenhofer in exchange for a look at the painting. When they finally enter Frenhofer's studio they discover a canvas filled with confusing lines and layers of paint—the work of a madman.

Frenhofer's own words betray him. "It's only the last stroke of the brush that counts.... No one gives us credit for what is underneath." He believes that with every stroke of the brush over the course of ten years, he has perfected his painting. Yet, when the other two artists observe a beautiful foot remaining in the corner of the canvas, "as ... Venus would appear among the ruins of a burned city," they recognize the destruction that has occurred. The master had laid down layer upon layer of paint upon his canvas believing that the last stroke was yet to come that would perfect his work. Instead, he had destroyed it.

Almost a century later, Pablo Picasso, commissioned to illustrate a special edition of this story, identified with Frenhofer. Perhaps he understood the pursuit of perfection or the consuming nature of putting one's own soul into a work. In a twist of fate, he happened to rent the studio where Balzac wrote the story and, there, he painted *Guernica*, which is referred to as his own "unknown masterpiece." One of the illustrations that Picasso drew for the Balzac story shows an artist working at a canvas filled with abstract lines and colors. His model is a woman knitting.

A woman came into Patternworks one day with a baby blanket that was beautifully knitted, worked in a lovely, soft yarn to be given as a gift at an upcoming baby shower. It was sweet and delicate. She was distressed. Twisting the blanket around, she showed me the cast-off edge and asked: "How can I make the cast-off edge exactly like the cast-on edge?" Given the cast-on method she had chosen, it was not possible to make a cast-off that looked exactly like it. She would have had to rip out and completely start anew, but I assured her that it was a beautiful work and would be appreciated. "But it doesn't match," she said. "What will the others say?" "They'll say it is great," I replied. But she didn't believe me and remained distressed, not able to see the beauty that lay between the cast-on and the cast-off. She left, frustrated that perfection had escaped her. I think she missed the point. Like Frenhofer, she thought that the last "stroke" of the cast-off was more important than what was underneath. She believed there was yet another last stroke that would bring perfection. When the pursuit of perfection drives the car, the passengers can get lost, and the journey is missed.

So, we have to be willing and realistic when a project disappoints. Remember that you have options: (1) rip it out; (2) give it away; (3) cut it up and make something else; (4) keep it for reference.

On Heeding the Wisdom of these Four Options

Option 1: Rip it out. The possibilities of ripping appealed to a gentleman who built wooden boats as a hobby and became a knitter after accompanying his wife to a class at a yarn shop. Woodworking offers no such forgiveness. Emi Nakamura, one of the participants in the Fushigi-noiroito project described in chapter 4, takes a philosophical approach. She writes: "The process of knitting almost always involves a positive (plus) action when the stitches increase and a negative (minus) action when parts are un-picked. One of the great attractions of knitting is how this characteristic process can be repeated at will. In the piece entitled 'Memories Held by Threads,' I focused on this minus action by showing examples of un-picked threads backed by photocopies of the knitted pieces of which they were formerly a part. The love and labor that I put into these pieces are held in the threads like a memory."[2] Ripping is an opportunity to reclaim the yarn for another project—an opportunity for a new beginning.

Option 2: Give it away. Elizabeth Zimmermann, in her wisdom, advised that if the sweater doesn't fit, give it to someone who does fit into it.

Option 3: Cut it up and make something else. One day I was struggling at my writing, stuck in a Google-researching rut, when I decided to go for a walk. Still no go. I broke for lunch, then picked up one of my knitting projects, a test of Janice's Cube That Wanted to Be a Ball pattern. I mused over the discussion we had had at our last meeting about the urge to make different sizes of these cubes from tiny to huge. Janice mentioned the possibility of using one of the fifty-pound capacity machines in the Laundromat to felt a giant version. I had also been thinking about cutting up unsuccessful or unfinished projects and piecing them together to make something else, in the spirit of this chapter, but believe it or not I couldn't find the pieces I had in mind when I looked. Instead, I had noticed the blah, beige, moth-eaten afghan that I had knit on the diagonal, like a dishcloth, using stripes of different pattern stitches. Unfortunately, in such a large piece, a one-directional diagonal skews to form a decidedly unpleasant shape, and the stitch patterns I chose were not bold enough to show up on the speckled yarn. So, sitting there, knitting a 6-inch cube, I suddenly thought of making a giant cube out of the afghan. I ran down to the basement and retrieved it.

I was surprised to find that it divided perfectly into the 6 sides I needed for the cube. With a big smile on my face, I cut it in half and then cut the halves into thirds. I laid out the 21-inch squares, alternating diagonal direction. I would normally leave a project like this for "tomorrow" and go back to my rut, but I was swept up in this adventure and was compelled to see it through to the end. I got some beige yarn and started sewing the pieces together with a backstitch. At first I felt rushed but noted how time didn't seem to be passing. I looked up at the clock several times and was surprised to see how much time I had, because the clock was hardly moving as I joined the pieces together. For a change, I had all the time I needed.

There were five CDs playing in random order and I was in heaven. When Barbara Streisand's *Higher Ground* came on, I was so happy to be alive that I actually cried, spun around, and danced. As I sewed, I wondered what to use to stuff this huge piece. The stack of old, smelly pillows in the basement came to mind. It took the fiberfill of two king-sized, one standard, and three euro pillows. Slitting them, transferring the stuffing to the cube, and disposing of the stained ticking was a pleasure and a service to the order of the basement.

Ready for the trip to the Laundromat, I carried my creation out to the car. It was then that I started to feel like I was in a Woody Allen movie. The cube was heavy and cumbersome, and extended beyond the top of the headrest, as it rode in the backseat. A parking space was waiting right in front of the Laundromat. As I carried in my strange laundry, I felt rather furtive. The attendant greeted me and, rather than stopping me, assisted in the process, but he asked if I was okay as I sat transfixed in front of the machine watching all sorts of spirals as the diagonals splashed around. The cube came out clean and sweet smelling, but it didn't shrink. I guess the agitation of a top-loading machine was necessary. When I got home, Marvin suggested I remove the stuffing and put the shell in my own washer. Great idea. It felted beautifully. There was now a wonderful, comfy floor pillow instead of an unloved afghan and a pile of rancid pillows. I acutely felt God's presence in the gift of that day. I wouldn't have been surprised to see a burning bush. Instead, we saw a perfect rainbow spread across the end of our road as we drove to join family for dinner.

Sue Bender in *Everyday Sacred* describes the way ceramic artist Kevin Nierman accidentally came by his signature "cracked pots." Nierman was horrified when a bowl he made for his friend Loie cracked. "This can't be. This can't crack ... after all the labor and love that went into it." But

Giant Ball: If you've knit lemons, make lemonade.

121

Loie said it reminded her of the mended teapots in the mountains of Pakistan, which were considered treasures. This was the permission Nierman needed. "Now I love cracking them.... I surrender to the destructive side, not knowing how the pot's going to come out. That side of me, the part that is very hard on myself, needed to be embraced.... It's trusting that it's going to work. Before, I would work and work and think I was on the right track, and then in the morning I'd think, 'How did the pots get so awful overnight?' Now something has shifted.... As soon as I was less critical of myself, I viewed the pots with different eyes.... Cracking pots served to melt my heart."[3] I was moved by this account and contacted Nierman about *The Knitting Way*. He kindly responded, "I guess trusting your process, listening carefully, and allowing it all to come together in words will be a big part of the process ... ah, sweet surrender!!"

Option 4: Keep it for reference. That's what many designers do. Mistakes create effects that may be useful in another project, making it a potential opportunity. It's also a way to see your progress. Perhaps this is a way to think about the Japanese concept of Wabi-Sabi, the aesthetic that finds solace in the simple and the natural, and respecting what *is*. It's about depth and space for transformation—not about external appearances, but the gradual appearance of inner essence. Beauty is defined by its imperfections. Leonard Koren, who wrote *Wabi-Sabi for Artists, Designers, Poets & Philosophers*, said in an interview by John Stark in *Body & Soul* magazine, "In order to see something, you have to offset it with a strong contrast. Let's say you have a primitive basket that is very imperfect. Put it in a seamless environment that doesn't have distractions—this is a good context to see it in. If everything is the same order of rusticity as the basket, you're not going to see the basket."

Once Again, It's All How You Look at It

Corrie Ten Boom was given the gift of seeing things differently. In February 1944, she and several family members were arrested in their homeland of Holland by the occupying German forces. This Christian family was charged by the Nazis with hiding Jews and helping them escape. Someone in the underground group that they worked through betrayed them. One of Ten Boom's experiences in the prison camps was being attacked by the never-ending infestation of fleas. Ten Boom questioned "why God had even made them." After a while, she and her sister, Betsy, were sent to the Ravensbrück concentration camp and both, being knitters, were given the task of knitting socks. It was a bit of a mystery to them why they and the other knitters of Barracks 28 were left totally unsupervised by the guards; in fact, Barracks 28 was never inspected, allowing Corrie and her sister to retain their Bible and vitamins (otherwise contraband). It was then revealed by one of the sock knitters that they were left alone because of the fleas! That's why the guards would not enter. So we see irritations can become blessings when given a different light. That's also part of "lightening up." This is not merely a weight factor but one of illumination. Twisting the way we see things, our knitting, the happenings in our lives, even our thinking can turn on the light of joy and delight and maybe even acceptance of ourselves.

For example, how do *you* feel about the fudge factor? It's our contention that most, if not all, experienced knitters, well, fudge. But you have to know yourself. If you tend toward "Oh, this isn't going to work" rigidity about options for fixes, then try a little fudging, but only if you can live with the results. Fudging isn't laziness. It's an economic move. It's a pragmatic move. (I'm having an irresistible urge toward fudge of the chocolate variety, right now.) Elizabeth Zimmermann, at one time, said that the only knitting mistake is a split stitch, because if you repeat what you thought was a mistake, it can become a design feature. Later, she even found a use for a split stitch (as an increase method). Another of EZ's wise observations was something like this: If a person riding by on a horse wouldn't notice your mistake, don't fret about it, unless it's right under your face.

Why do some features of a finished project bother you? Maybe it's because you know too much! Become like a little child. Put aside your critical voice and respect yourself enough to "hang that sweater on the refrigerator like a child's piece of art." Fix what you can fix, especially if you discover the mistake when it's completely finished. Do what you can do and let it go. Let's say you find a dropped stitch way back. There are options. You can ladder down and work it back up. You can tack it down, anchoring it so that it doesn't ravel. If it just involves a couple of rows, it may be better to rip. Be at peace with your work.

What are your rules? "I only knit with natural fibers," "I only knit with bulky yarns," "I never use straight needles (or circular)." Examine your rules. Try avoiding the rules. Break the rules. Take a peek outside your box and jump out. Allow yourself to risk freedom. Allow yourself a luxury now and then. Allow yourself to lighten up and be open to serendipity.

It's said that serendipity, the unexpected discovery that pops up just when you need it, has been an important contributor to the progress of science. Social scientist Robert K. Merton, who identified the "serendipity pattern in scientific inquiry," stressed that serendipity doesn't produce discoveries, but provides opportunities for discoveries, openings. Serendipity certainly has played a big part in the unfolding of my life. For example, when Patternworks was less than a year old, I was trying to follow a slip-stitch pattern from a stitch treasury. I misread the pattern and stumbled into double knitting, which was important in the growth of Patternworks. Just by knitting and slipping across the row in a certain way (not what the directions intended), there were suddenly two layers of fabric with a cozy air space between! I imagined a knitted version of the popular down vest. We published the pattern, #801, in 1980. Its popularity helped jump-start Patternworks.

Do you make time to be silly, playful? When *was* the last time you twirled around in your living room?

And do you ever act from whimsy—"unpredictably and more from whim or caprice than from reason or judgment," as defined by *Webster's Dictionary*—giving in to impulse? I can only imagine designer Michael Kors's state of mind when he created the "Lavender Dyed Knitted Mink Poncho" sold at Bloomingdales for $7,825. And how about the knitter? You couldn't knit thick strips of mink on a knitting machine, could you? Looks to be about 2 stitches or less to an inch. And I can only imagine why the model in the ad looked more nauseated than tickled by the poncho and its long mink fringe on her bare skin. In the spirit of silliness, Janice says, "How about creating a poncho for a mink to wear? Okay, how about for the cat?"

Space between the Loops
Knitting Outside the Ball

It all began when my friend went to Ghana to work in a mission school. When she left, I presented her with two balls of cotton sock yarn and a set of double point needles. She took them to Kumasi, and her knitting became a curiosity to the young women there at the school. They wanted to learn to knit, and it set me to thinking about the unavailability of wool yarn, or perhaps any kind of yarn, in near-equatorial Africa, and what materials could be substituted for yarn. Thinking outside the box, I brought this idea of other knitting possibilities to my comfortable American home.

I remembered Mary, with whom I worked at Pattern-works. She taught someone to knit at a wedding reception using the ribbon from the flower centerpieces and straws as needles. Ribbon appealed to me, but there's plenty of manufactured ribbon yarn. Then one day on a trip to the craft store, I came across a large spool of shiny fuchsia-colored "curling" ribbon. It is the kind used to decorate gifts—the kind you run a scissor blade over to bring about ringlet "curlies." I took it home and knit a small coin purse, just to see if it would work. It did! It was a girlie color that made me envision a wonderful floppy hat for my granddaughter, Isabella. Now inspiration came because I remembered those funny poodles made from the plastic bags that covered the dry cleaning and little rugs crocheted out of plastic bread wrappers. (Thank you, mom, for the Pac-O-Fun legacy!) This ribbon did have a decidedly plastic feel. It was plastic, not paper, as I had thought. I tested it in water to make sure it wouldn't disintegrate. Isabella's hat came along, but as I worked the beginning of the crown, I was perplexed that the piece seemed to want to stay flat, instead of building up as a "tube." But I persisted and it soon presented itself like a bright pink flower bud, the brim ruffling like the edges of an iris. What a pleasant surprise! I'm pretty confident that no yarn would have given the same effect. What fun!

What grown-up lady wouldn't feel like a little girl again in this fun chapeau? Make one for the little girl in your life—or in you. Let your inner child show herself again as you make this sweet flower of a hat. Think about the free spirit inside you.

Experience It for Yourself

Curly Ribbon Hat

¼-inch curling ribbon such as used in gift wrapping.

I found a spool of 500 yards of this type of ribbon at a nationally known craft store. *Note:* It is recommended that you test your ribbon in water, because some of these do disintegrate when they come in contact with water.

I used size US 8 16-inch circular needles and approximately 250 yards of curling ribbon. You will also need same size double point needles (DPNs) to complete the top of the hat.

Gauge: 18 stitches equals 4 inches. Remember that this will not stretch like wooly yarn.

Size is for small (medium, large) child's head. I made the small and it fits a two-year-old.

Cast on 160 (176, 192) stitches. Join. Knit 1 round. Purl 1 round.

Knit 10 (12, 14) rounds.

Next round: Knit 2 together all around—80 (88, 96) stitches now on the needles.

Knit straight until length from the knit 2 together round is 5 (6, 7) inches (or as deep as you would like the crown of the hat). Now begin decreases for the top of hat.

Round 1: *Knit 8 (9, 10), Knit 2 together. Repeat from *

Rounds 2, 4, 6, 8, 10: Knit.

Round 3: Knit 7 (8, 9), Knit 2 together. Repeat till the end of round.

Round 5: Knit 6 (7, 8), Knit 2 together. Repeat till the end of round.

Round 7: Knit 5 (6, 7), Knit 2 together. Repeat till the end of round.

Round 9: Knit 4 (5, 6), Knit 2 together. Repeat till the end of round.

Round 11: Knit 3 (4, 5), Knit 2 together. Repeat till the end of round. At about this point you will need to change to the DPNs, and you are working decreases every round.

Curly Ribbon Hat and Purse: A party on and from your needles.

127

Round 12: Knit 2 (3, 4), Knit 2 together. Repeat till the end of round.

Round 13: Knit 1 (2, 3), Knit 2 together. Repeat till the end of round.

Continue as established, decreasing every round until 8 stitches remain. Draw the ribbon through the 8 stitches and pull up tight. Weave in ends and embellish with ribbons, buttons, or crocheted flowers, if you like.

Experience It for Yourself

This little pocket is a small reminder that we are containers of a valuable commodity: our souls.

Curly Ribbon Coin Purse (or Prayer Pocket)

Using size US 3 needles, cast on 12 stitches and work in garter stitch for 4 inches.

Make the fold-over flap. Knit 1, knit 2 together, knit remaining stitches every row until 5 stitches remain.

Next Row: Knit 2, yarn over, knit 2 together, knit 1. Buttonhole made.

Continue: Knit 1, knit 2 together, knit remaining stitches every row until 2 stitches remain. Bind off. Fold cast-on edge up to the beginning of the fold-over flap and sew side seams. Fold flap over and attach a small button as a closure.

What else could be used to knit with? Rope, string, licorice whips, cooked spaghetti, tall Pampas grass, and what about strips of cloth? Rags would work, but lovely calico yard goods would be pleasing and appear more "planned," if that is even a good thing. I bought 2.5 yards and, following a cutting method that I found for cutting fabric to make twined rugs, I ended up with a continuous 1-inch strip of about 100 hundred yards. I cut it on the straight grain (see Diagram for Cutting Fabric into a Continuous Strip) but also suggest trying to cut on the cross grain or on the bias. Using very large needles and large gauge, I knitted a rectangle, which makes a very nice mat for a table. More yardage would make a rustic rug for the floor. I can see it used in garments, for bags, for hats, or, using fleece, a warm hat and scarf set, and a vest with bigger needles and stockinette stitch.

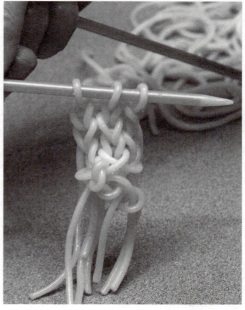

Spaghetti: (1) Knit.
(2) Eat.

Experience It for Yourself

Purchase your choice of fabric. If it is cotton, I recommend preshrinking it. Lay it out on a large surface (I used the floor) and with very sharp scissors, cut it into a continuous strip following the diagram. I "eyeballed" it and tried to keep my strip near 1 inch wide. Roll into a ball, then knit as with any yarn. I used US 11 needles and got a gauge of 10 stitches equals 4 inches. Casting on 30 stitches, I just knit in garter stitch until I ran out of material.

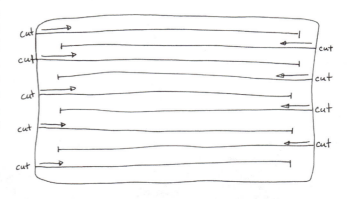

Cutting fabric into a continuous strip.

So, the Knitting Way involves whimsy, serendipity, play, "lightening up," letting go, and expansion. There's lots of joy on the Way. Are you having fun yet?

Space between the Loops
Knitting Goes to the Dog

There are certain inherent dangers when one owns a dog.

It all started with not having enough yarn to knit a pair of socks where each sock would be the same. It came to me that if I worked the socks as negatives of each other, I would have a pair of socks that would match, but not match. So, with a ball of red and a ball of blue yarn, I knitted the first sock with a red cuff, blue leg, red heel, blue foot, red toe. Then, reversing the colors for the second sock, I proceeded with a blue cuff, red leg, blue heel, red foot, blue toe. How pleased I was with myself and my creativity and thriftiness, for the yarn was all used up.

Then the dog ate the sleeve of my ready-made Dale Norwegian cardigan. Horrors! These are not cheap sweaters, and to fix the cuff would require working at a very small gauge—that is, if I could even find the right yarn to repair it. I was able to acquire the replacement yarn from Dale of Norway and, after some (yikes) cutting, trimming, a pattern change and tiny-gauge knitting, new cuffs were added.

But the dog was not finished. Coming home from work, I discovered that this dog had done it again. He had eaten the tops of a pair of red sparkling socks that I had made. Now you're probably saying, "Why can't she just keep things out of the dog's reach?" and you would be right in your assessment. Anyway, I had just enough yarn to re-knit the cuffs of those socks, that is, if I made the legs much shorter, creating anklets.

Not long after this repair job, my previously mentioned negative socks fell victim to the canines of

A new way with fabric.

the resident canine. Yes, the toes and feet were chewed off this time. I gave up. I had no yarn to fix them and it seemed to me that sometimes you just have to let go. Was I being told something? *Dog* spelled backwards is *god.* The idea of the negative socks knocked around in my head for quite awhile.

Then it hit me: Take four colors and knit four socks. If you use the same pattern in each sock and rearrange the colors—you get four pairs of socks: Quad Socks. They match, but they don't exactly match. Each sock goes with any of the other socks, so four socks make four pairs. (You can really make six possible pairs, and you can put the four colors together in even more combinations to make even more "matching" socks, but then we couldn't call them Quad Socks.) Do you see the other configurations?

The morals of the story are: It's often good to not have enough yarn, and sometimes you need to let go.

Experience It for Yourself

These are a treat, like candy, and just plain fun. Open yourself to letting the fun come in. You are encouraged to think about other patterns and color combinations. Make sure you flaunt these by wearing them with clogs or sandals!

Janice's Quad Socks

For these socks I chose a light worsted weight yarn, sometimes called double knit or DK weight. You will need 4 different colors (A, B, C, D)—approximately 133 yards each. You may need more if you have a long foot. (I wear a size 6½ shoe.) I used size US 4 double point needles (DPNs) and achieved a gauge of 5.5 stitches equals 1 inch. (*Note:* I'm a loose knitter. You may need larger needles to get that gauge.) These socks are knitted in the round. Directions are for the first sock's color way (with changes for each of the other socks in parentheses.)

Cuff and Leg

With color A (B, C, D), cast on 40 stitches onto 3 needles, and working in the round, knit 2, purl 2, until piece measures 2 inches. Now begin knitting every round. Change to color B (C, D, A) and knit 3 rounds. With color C (D, A, B), knit 3 rounds. Repeat these 6 rounds, 1 time.

Next round—Knit 1 round in color A (B, C, D).

Next 2 rounds: *Knit 2 in color A (B, C, D), knit 2 in color D (A, B, C), repeat from * around.

Next 2 rounds: *Knit 2 in color D (A, B, C), knit 2 in color A (B, C, D), repeat from * around.

Next 2 rounds: *Knit 2 color A (B, C, D), knit 2 color D (A, B, C), repeat from * around.

Next round: Knit 1 round color A (B, C, D).

Quad Socks: Think outside the socks!

Knit 3 rounds with color C (D, A, B), knit 3 rounds with color B (C, D, A).

Repeat these 6 rounds 1 time.

Heel Flap

With color A (B, C, D), knit across 20 stitches onto one needle. These will be heel flap stitches. Divide remaining stitches evenly across the other 2 needles. Hold these stitches aside while working on the heel flap. Turn the heel flap needle, wrong side facing, and slipping the first stitch, purl across (you will now be working back and forth). Turn. Right side showing. Always slip the first stitch of every row.

Row 1 (right side) of heel flap: Slip 1, *knit 1, slip l. Continue across entire row from *. End with knit 1.

Row 2 (wrong side) of heel flap: Slip 1, purl across.

Repeat these 2 rows for 20 rows. End with a wrong side row.

Turn Heel

Note: *psso* means "pass the slipped stitch over" the just knitted stitch.

With right side facing, knit 12, slip 1, knit 1, psso, k1. Turn.

Slip the first stitch, purl 5, purl 2 together, purl 1. Turn.

Slip the first stitch, knit 6, slip1, knit 1, psso, knit 1. Turn.

Slip the first stitch, purl 7, purl 2 together, purl 1. Turn.

Slip the first stitch, knit 8, slip1, knit 1, psso, knit 1. Turn.

Slip the first stitch, purl 9, purl 2 together, purl 1. Turn.

Slip the first stitch, knit 10, slip1, knit 1, psso. Turn.

Slip the first stitch, purl 10, purl 2 together. Turn. 12 stitches are on the needle.

Instep

With color D (A, B, C), knit across the 12 stitches on the needle. Pick up 11 stitches across the previously slipped stitches on the left side of the heel flap—needle #1. With needle #2, knit across the 20 stitches that you have held aside. With needle #3, pick up 11 stitches across the previously slipped edge stitches on the right side of the heel flap and knit 6 stitches from the heel. You will have 17 stitches on needle #1, 20 stitches on needle #2, and 17 stitches on needle #3. Knit 1 round plain.

Next round: Knit to within 3 stitches of the end of needle #1. Knit 2 together, knit 1.

Knit across needle #2 (this needle will always have 20 stitches).

Needle #3—knit 1, slip1, knit 1, psso, knit to the end of the needle.

Next round: Knit one round plain.

Repeat these two rounds until needle #1 has 10 stitches, needle #2 has 20 stitches and needle #3 has 10. Total of 40 stitches.

Continue knitting around plain to within 2 inches of the total foot length from the back of the heel. Example: Foot measures a total of 9 inches, sock at this point should measure 7 inches from the back of the heel.

Change to color B (C, D, A) and knit 1 round.

Next 2 rounds: *Knit 2 of color C (D, A, B); knit 2 of color B (C, D, A); repeat from * around.

Knit 1 round B (C, D, A).

Toe

Change to color A (B, C, D) and knit one round.

Toe decreases on the next round as follows.

Round 1: Needle #1—knit to within 3 stitches of the end, knit 2 together, knit 1.

Needle #2—knit 1, slip1, knit 1, psso, knit to within 3 stitches of the end, knit 2 together, knit 1.

Needle #3—knit 1, slip 1, k1, psso, knit to the end.

Round 2: Knit plain.

Repeat these two rounds until a total of 20 stitches remain. Repeat Round 1 only until a total of 8 stitches remain.

Finish off by running the tail of yarn through the last 8 stitches and drawing up, or you may graft these stitches together. Now make 3 more socks, changing the color way as indicated.

Children know how to play. We all did at one time. No one needs to teach children how to feel free, to run and jump and live with imagination. Our first learning came through an innate sense of wonder and curiosity. Playfulness still exists in even the most serious adult, but it doesn't come out unless we allow it to. Letting playfulness emerge through our knitting—by freeing ourselves from perfection and rules—may be a new, and highly recommended, experience for some of us. Childlike faith is a blessed state of seeing and being, and we all would benefit from a little bit of that—along with some silliness, whimsy, and joy every day.

6

Making a Daily Practice
Cultivating the Time for Knitting

Knitting (for Dino)

Alighting westward
in the grey dawn
you gained seven hours, like seven stitches cast on:
*   unnoticing, passed through*
time zones and customs checks
grit-eyed and dreaming, with a freight of gifts.

Returning eastward, wrenched
Against the sun,
after five days
your brother's wedding
family meeting, parting—
filled to the brim
with special dishes, drinking, love and tears
and then squeezed tight, so tight—

undone tasks
wait for you at the airport
a hangover of carelessly invited
unwanted grumbling guests.
Seven hours slip off
the flashing needles, as the wool pulls taut—
one plain, one purl, knit two, knit three together—
clicking your frantic knitting against time
where gaps like this, dropped stitches

let in the daylight.
This is a pattern only you could make.

You once lent me
One of these sweaters of your own design.
Over my shoulders, sleeves
casually tied in front, it kept me warm
through harsh winter.

—Pauline Burton, in *OutLoud*[1]

The Resting Place

Having enough time to knit was always a big issue with knitters who came through the doors—and the telephone lines—of Patternworks. God knows it has been one of my issues. Cottage Creations even designed a coffee mug emblazoned with the slogan "So much yarn, so little time" under a cartoon of a harried knitter running full tilt, dragging a half-knitted scarf and a ball of yarn. Time doesn't care about our schedules or our needs. There's nothing new about this, although we have sped up considerably since 1938 when Mary Thomas commented in *Mary Thomas's Knitting Book*, "Knitting should be done thoughtfully. It should not be hurried. That is its charm to our generation, who live surrounded with a wild helter-skelter of speed."

"Time is vanishing because we have lost the practice of consciously inhabiting our life.... It is not more time, more days and years, that we are starved for, it is *the present moment*," writes Jacob Needleman, presenting the teaching of the wisdom traditions in *Time and the Soul*. "Only fools—fools like us—think we can 'manage' the great river of time. Time flows through us and is spent in our thoughts and feelings and sensations.... We need to *feel* the question of time much more deeply and simply than we do.... [Time] can only be given ... to try to get time, is as futile as trying to get happiness, that happiness which is not pleasure but an abiding sense of meaning and well-being. Such things are given, not taken. But in order to receive, the hand needs to be open."[2]

Here's another paradox. First we must *find* the time that has been given to come to our knitting. Once we're there, we can practice. Getting, or being, there is the first step. This remains a stumbling block for me when I come to a crunch, as I'm racing the deadline to finish this book. Now, when I need my daily practice more than ever, I skip it, supposedly to make time for writing. I know better, but my hands are clenched.

Okay. I'm considering what Maurice Nicoll in *Living Time and the Integration of the Life* calls the "already-thereness" of everything. Like an insect crawling on a tree who doesn't know the leaves are already there waiting for him to reach them, our "road is there but we do not necessarily go along it but may walk round and round the same point unable to escape from the circle of our habits."[3] What I need to say is already there.

According to the Bible, Nicoll explains, God—defined as "the beginning and the end" and "all possibilities"—created aeon (*olam* in Hebrew) containing all things and all possibilities. The normal way we experience time—one thing happening after another—is one dimensional, like a line. He tells us the time lines of our lives are like threads (let's think strands of yarn). There's a strand of yarn for everyone. Nicoll asks us to imagine all these time lines, each strand of yarn, with each part of its length drawn through "higher space" to another dimension. "Now we have to imagine that this higher space contains everything—all possibilities, all possible events, all possible experiences, the sum total of reality known and unknown. Consider one thought developed [or one stitch knit] ... into every possible result and every conceivable form ... the infinite expression, the infinite form of this thought [or stitch] ... [but] time as we know it suffers from insufficiency. It has not the dimensional capacity to contain aeon." My writing is coming easier.

Imagine that you are a drawing of yourself, living on a sheet of paper. You know only two dimensions, left and right, up and down. You have no knowledge of above and below, the third dimension you experience as a human on earth. To you, as a drawing, nothing exists above or below. So, imagine what you see when the paper is pierced by a yarn needle and a strand of yarn is drawn through—some sort of attack of flashing lines (cross sections of the needle), then a series of fibrous invasions. Unbeknownst to you, as a drawing, the length of time the "attack" and "invasion" took was determined by the lengths of the needle and yarn, which exist outside the world of your experience. You can only connect to the reality of the event by recognizing that there's a dimension you cannot see.

As humans, we have no problem understanding that two events exist simultaneously in space. You're reading this book at the same time someone is knitting in Japan. Your house exists before you enter it and after you leave it. But, as humans, it takes a leap of faith to recognize another dimension where the "already thereness" of everything exists.

Nicoll goes on to say that there's also an "inner space," which is our emotional state. "The state of suspicion, for instance, is [a] *place* which has its own properties. When we are in that state, we can study the properties of this place in inner space, if we have sufficient detachment.... The transition to the state of joy will mean movement to another place in inner space having quite different properties.... We continually come to the same *places* without fully recognizing them. Psychologically, we must always be *somewhere* in inner space—just as we must be in outer space.... In *now* we get above state. Inner space is changed, enlarged."[4] It's true. Now, with an hour left before Janice comes, I somehow feel I have more time to get this down than I did all weekend sitting in front of the keyboard.

What's more, time and space are inseparable. In her online article "Holding the Space, A Doula's Best Gift,"

Pam England, a nurse-midwife, tells the story of a "knitting midwife ... whose unusual form of labor support was sitting in the corner of the room and knitting." England points out that in relation to giving birth, "Whatever its form, genuine support comes from a positive intention to 'hold the space for the mother' in the belief that she is moment-by-moment discovering how to birth." Rather than making her seem unavailable, the knitting created a protective container of comfort and assurance. One mother said, "So long as she was knitting, I knew nature and I were still on course."[5]

This combined time/space concept comes more naturally to people in Asia, according to Japanese Professor Mitsuhiro Takemura. Water clocks from China work by filling a vessel-contained space with the flow of water in time. The Japanese Tea Ceremony, with its disciplined form capturing the time/space concept of *ma* or "interval," provides a sacred space and time for a human encounter, a reminder that each moment here will never recur exactly the same way again.

I'm still not always able to find such a space, although brewing tea seems to make intervals appear. In the few minutes while the kettle boils, and the five minutes the tea brews, I find the space to sail through a job that begs doing.

Janice says, "One must access time and then act in it." I asked her for an example. "Sometimes we have the sense that there is no time to get anything done. But we aren't taking advantage of the small time places (holding spaces) in our life. The other night I was preparing a ravioli dinner for the family. The sauce was made and it was time to boil up the water to cook the ravioli. Note that I need to use a very large pot for the six to eight or more people who can be in my house on any given night. Waiting for water to boil is a small time place, unless it's a large pot; then it's a little bit larger than a small time place. While I waited, I was able to knit a few rounds on a small slipper that I am making for my grandson. I moved about from the table to standing at the stove with my yarn ball hidden in my left armpit. It was not a great stretch of knitting but I felt a sense of time fulfillment. These small moments, when added up, can make for a good deal of time just waiting to be accessed and acted upon. It is gratifying to take advantage of them."

Janice also tells the story of how her knitting helps her hold the space for her grandson, little Ryan, when he takes his nap. "At the same time every day, 1:45, we pick a book. I say, 'It's afternoon rest time and we're just going to sit here quietly. If you feel sleepy, just lay down on the pillow. Do you feel sleepy? (Um hum.) Do you want a blanket? (Um hum.) Do you want me to sit here with you and knit while you rest? (Um hum.) It's a ritual for him. He doesn't have to fight going to sleep. Grandma isn't going anywhere."

Isn't that what life's about? Focused on holding the space that's needed for whatever needs to unfold, we can't worry about passing time. The Bible seems to address knitters directly with advice from the book of Matthew (6:19–21) that uses the moth as a symbol of the passing of time: "Lay not up for yourselves treasures upon earth, where moth and rust doth corrupt, and where thieves break through and steal. But lay up for yourselves treasures in heaven, where neither moth nor rust doth corrupt, and where thieves do not break through and steal. For where your treasure is, there will your heart be."

Space between the Loops
Hearing the Rhythm

When I was little girl growing up in Florida, my sister and three brothers and I played in an empty lot two streets away from our house. It was a cul-de-sac that jutted out into a canal. Almost totally surrounded by water, it had several half-buried two-by-four planks of wood that hung out over the water, and we called the place "Shipwreck Island." We imagined that we were shipwrecked and had to live off the land like pirates or Robinson Crusoe. We packed lunches and were gone all day. None of us owned a watch—how could pirates like us tell time? Under the influence of the cartoon character Fred Flintstone, we constructed small sundial wristwatches out of cardboard and old watchbands. Of course, our prehistoric watches didn't tell time, but we children felt the time by the angles of the sun and shadows. We always seemed to get home in time for dinner.

Most of us grew up to live our lives tied to the clock. The Greenwich Mean Time tone broadcast on public radio tells us the correct time to set our life to. The clock radio is what wakes us, the digital watch shines out the numbers to the second, and we live our lives to the alarms of our PDAs—personal digital assistants. We know about the sun and moon, planets, galaxies, and black holes, but we have lost our hold on the rhythms of sunrise, sunset, constellations, and seasons.

My grandfather was a farmer. He worked his land until he was well into his nineties. At the beginning of each year he placed a new calendar directly on top of the old one so that several years of calendars dangled on a long nail in the wall near the kitchen table. Every day— *every day*—he marked down the weather in each day's space. His life was lived to the seasons, and his calendars were about the sunrise, the temperature, the rainfall or lack thereof, storms, and beautiful days. They—not time— marked the rhythm of season and weather.

Knitting has a rhythm, too. It will mark time if you let it. Not as a clock but as an almanac of your life. It will allow you to slow to the broader rhythm of seasons, rather than the narrow swing of the pendulum. Knitting has the capacity to contain the times of your life. One stitch made is more valuable than the time it took.

In the book of Genesis (1:14) God said, "Let there be lights in the expanse of the sky to separate the day from the night and let them serve as signs to mark seasons and days and years." And Psalm 104 reminds us that "The moon marks off the seasons and the sun knows when to go down." God didn't proclaim, "Let there be clocks to mark the time."

As I said, I don't always find the access to my space and time, as strange as that sounds, so I enjoy hearing how other people handle the issue. Tomi, the member of my community knitting group who knit the Log Cabin Square samples, has a daily practice of knitting in the morning, and she was inspired for a period of years to keep a log of the times she knit. Her notebook is filled with entries, such as: "2/12/03 8:45–9:15, 3:10–3:20, 7:30–8:30." I believe she also included an identifier for what she was working on at the time, such as "Blue Aran." Isn't that great! It reminds me of the visual record of Japanese artist On Kawara's Today Series exhibit at the Dia Museum in Beacon, New York. Kawara created a poster-size time-line calendar with dots painted to indicate days he created one of the paintings in the series. His rule: Each painting (which was the date written out in the language and custom of the country he was in at the time) could take only one day, or he destroyed it. I thought, wouldn't such an exercise—an expanse of the year(s) in plain sight—with a dot for each day I knit—give a picture of my progress on the path? Maybe, different colors to indicate ... Wait a minute. I haven't started it yet because I tend to complicate things. Tomi simply started recording her log that marked the days in a plain notebook. No thinking, just doing from the inner center.

I bought a beautiful van Gogh datebook at an after-holiday sale last year to help me write a few lines every morning when I get up, since I had been so erratic with my "morning pages," prescribed by Julia Cameron in *The*

Artist's Way. This, of course, wasn't the answer ... because there isn't an answer. I know it's a state of mind and a place, already there, that I'm slowly moving to.

Space between the Loops
Tips on Daily Practice

Daily practice begins with an attitude. Recognize whether you're feeling humbly grateful or grumbly hateful. An attitude of thankfulness is an opening. Thankfulness for hands and yarn, for soul and mind and imagination—all are gifts. Breathing is a gift. To choose to be grateful for the gifts of your life can set the tone of your daily practice. It keeps us in a place of humble openness to receive the benefits of life and joy and peace. Give thanks for your joy in the pleasure of your knitting. Give thanks for the working of your hands and your heart. Attitude is a choice. Sometimes you come with a bad attitude. Acknowledge that you have a need to be made whole.

Another step toward this daily practice goal is having a place for it. A place that is yours, a place that no one will bother, is best, and size doesn't have to matter. Even a chair, a corner, or a closet will do (although I've been in closets bigger than my bedroom). What matters is a place of consistency. That's how habits are formed, through the consistent doing of a thing. I wish I could say that I had a whole room in my house that I could dedicate to this aspect of my life, but I do not. I have two places. One is for the daily intake, the disciplined study and reading of my Bible and the writings of others; one is for the knitting and reflection upon what has been my daily spiritual intake. The former is my kitchen table; the latter is my living room sofa, near the good light and my knitting corner. Using these places consistently has trained my mind and thoughts and hands to be upon the things that matter. I believe the kitchen to be the heart of the home and a place where family connections can come alive. My own relationship with God is one of family and it is only natural for us to get together over tea, so that I may learn. Nearsightedness and the need for bifocals have also necessitated the use of a table for my books! It's just easier. Being comfortable to knit is paramount. Physical aches and pains will come quickly for me, otherwise, and the sofa is the best place I have, at this time. The family objected so severely to my previous chair that I relented and got rid of it (it *was* a hideous orange and the caning on the sides *was* splitting—no, shredding apart—but it was *so* comfortable).

Prepare and pour yourself a cup of tea. What is it about tea that naturally goes with knitting? I like my coffee, but tea goes with knitting. Remember the tea parties of your childhood? The event was so special, surrounded by your friends, your dollies and bears all enjoying the miniature china tea set (the one with the pink roses) acting grown-up and polite. Tea for one is just as enjoyable. Boil the water, warm the pot, measure the leaves, wait for the steeping and pour. Steam rises from the pretty cups, warming the hands, warming the insides, warming the soul. The knitting steeps, the pretty yarns, warm the hands, warm the body, and warm the soul. Needles meet like two friends embracing. Tea can be ritual, ceremony. Knitting can be ritual, ceremony. Teas are used for celebration and healing. Knitting is celebratory and healing. I sit with my knitting and sip my tea. They comfort and provide health benefits. Taste and aroma fill the senses and added to the touch and sight of knitting, the clickity clack of the needles, you have a total sensory experience. This total experience can create a comforting and settling place for the knitting.

So, now that you have a place, and perhaps a cup of tea, it's time to set yourself up for success. Discouragement is insidious, creeping and seeping in, so don't make it easy for this saboteur. Have the things you need nearby to make yourself successful. If you are sitting down to knit and you must keep popping up to retrieve another ball of yarn or markers or scissors, you will soon grow weary and distracted. Provide for yourself the means of having what you need right there within your reach. What good is it to have all the gadgets in the world, yet not where you can get at them easily? A basket, a box, a shelf, or a bag—use whatever it takes. I actually keep several zippered pouches filled with the gadgets needed, each one in a separate basket or bag so that I don't have to continually search and move a single pouch from project to project. I'm so glad God gave us zipper-seal bags! I organize my smaller projects in these little wonders (yes, I have many more than one project going at a time) in order to grab them easily when the mood strikes for a particular one.

I encourage you to seek out the writings and wisdom of your own traditions, both the spiritual teachings and the knitting traditions. This is another way of moving toward success. Ancient and contemporary writers have wisdom. Look for those who give their wisdom generously. The generous spirit of another will only add to yours. Have these voices nearby and available. I have found that the voice of another can bring new ways of looking at things, new methods and insights. To neglect this wisdom is a disservice to yourself.

Make this place and time conducive to your spiritual explorations. Light a candle, if you like. There is something so lovely in candlelight, and darkness does not overcome it. Even in the darkest place, a flame cannot be extinguished by the darkness. Light always overcomes the dark. A candle symbolizes that no matter what darkness may be at play in your life, there is still hope and goodness and understanding. I love to burn candles in my kitchen, when I cook or do the dishes. A candle evokes and invokes a welcome presence. Candles represent warmth, security, safety, and home. A candle burning in the window says, "You are welcome, come home." God is light, and contemplating the flame while knitting is connection. I will add one cautionary note—personal experience has taught me that candlelighting is not a good idea around the sweeping tail of a cat or dog.

Adding music to your space may be attractive to you as well. Music has power and points to the eternal. Like knitting, there is color and texture in music. It is a good companion to have along with your knitting. Like knitting, music is subjective. We knitters all have our favorite yarns and styles. The kind of tunes and melodies one person loves is cacophony to another. I have to be careful about my choice of music, as I am prone to leave the world of the knitter and enter the world of the musician. It's a bit of a struggle for me sometimes, so I generally choose instrumental music (otherwise I will want to sing along) and no guitar-driven music (otherwise I will want to analyze and play along). I can't go wrong with Mozart! Piano concertos and people singing in Latin are safe. Maybe heavy-metal speaks to you. Music can give you a double dose of opening space inside. It brings about another road of awareness that can smooth out your knitting path, two roads that run parallel and in harmony with each other.

Need I say, if this time is to be your spiritual connection time, turn off the TV? That is only competition for your thoughts, your brain. I don't say, "Never knit with the TV on," just limit the TV when you are being spiritually purposeful with your knitting. Being selfish with your soul is a good thing. Guard it from anything that would steal it away.

Be alone. Solitude brings experience. There seems to be a prevailing theme among the spiritual teachings of the past and the present and that is the theme of "wilderness." Not necessarily the literal wilderness—walking out into a desert—but to leave the comforts of life, the companionship of others for a time, heightens the experience of the Holy. A retreat gives the opportunity for just such an experience. It allows for focus and total immersion into the moments of communion with the Divine. Attending planned retreats at religious institutions is certainly an option, but you can learn to create daily retreats for your soul. A brief prayer, the acknowledgment of the beauty that falls upon you, the sublime leaving of the moments around you to rise above them—these are moments of choosing and holding onto the Transcendent. This is retreat. This is quality, bonding time with the Holy, still and listening, alone but not lonely. Insight will come from others in your life—you should expect that—but the alone time will train you to really listen. Solitude is a teacher. There is a time for social knitting and there is spiritual benefit in that, but the alone time makes the together time better. When you learn to listen in your alone time, you will hear God all the better when you are with others, and you will listen all the better to others.

And this is the one that makes Linda weep ...

Keep a journal. Writing down the "who" of you is one of the most valuable things you can do for yourself. Journaling brings things to your awareness that you may not have considered, things that you may have not seen. It serves as a record of your life and thoughts. My knitting journal and my journaling are about me—my projects and ideas. It keeps me honest about myself and is a boon to remembering what I did and learned in my knitting. It also marks the times of my life as I add notes about the people that I knit for. That's one of the things I like the best, going back over my notes and remembering the people I have knitted for. I'm a real sucker for any of the myriad blank books that are available today at all the bookstores. Choose one that will entice you to write in it. Choose one that you want to touch, that feels good in your hands, one that says, "Don't forget me." Choose one that will contain you lovingly.

Certain types of projects may be more conducive to this way of embracing your knitting as a spiritual place. Again we have the freedom of subjectivity. Some speak of those long stretches of plain knitting as "mindless," but I have grown to not care for that word. I know that it means that your concentration doesn't have to hold itself to the work in your hands, but the knitting certainly is not mindless. I think that it is truly mindful. How sneaky of this plain knitting to be so smooth going, so tranquil that you are lulled into the depth and fullness of your mind! Still others appreciate the rhythm of Fair Isle with its little singsong way of keeping to the pattern, 3 red, 2 blue, 3 red, 2 blue. This repetition also has the power to expose the depths for some. I seem to choose the sock project for my depth plumbing. Socks are formulaic and have an easily marked structure: cuff, leg, heel, foot, toe. Knitting in the round is satisfying and there is just something wonderful about wool socks on the feet (especially in my drafty old farmhouse in February). Then there are those long stretches of the body of a sweater or the gentle sloping sleeves. Those are good potentials for me. Knitters seem to know what kind of knitting really leads them into a spiritual experience. If you don't yet know, try one, then another until your discovery happens. Be aware of your comfort level. Why suffer? In a challenge, there's growth at the end. I tried the challenge of intarsia and did not grow with it, although I suffered. But things are different at different times.

Sitting down and taking up this way of knitting, of thinking about your knitting, has unexpected pleasures and benefits. Being spiritually purposeful in this daily practice is worth the effort it takes. Be still in your mind and spirit, breathe and listen. Wait and create and say, "Thank you. That was good."

Make it easy to be successful. Prepare for the next session. This clears confusion and keeps you from making excuses to avoid your practice. For self-protection and motivation, make time and effort to tidy up so next time you pick up your knitting it's ready to go. Such things as winding balls, photocopying the pattern so you can mark it up with your notes and progress, pinning tags to your knitting for reminder notes—so you don't need to rely on the famous last words "I'll remember." Keep your knitting in an accessible place. Cleaning up after a project clears away the past to make way for the present.

Be kind to yourself. I confess that I've gone through periods, some during the writing of this book, when I didn't knit daily. The chaos of my life takes over in such a way these days that I can't seem to find the moment for my own time. (Could this just be an excuse?) My household has become a hub of crazy activity, and I seem to get taken over by other cares at this time. Someone once said, "Life is what happens when you're making other plans." It's hard to admit this as someone who is trying to write a book on spirituality. How can I speak with conviction when I seem to be lagging in my own daily practice? But that is where grace comes in. I ask for grace. Every day truly is a new beginning.

How I Get Inside My Knitting

I start by getting physically comfortable. How often do we sit or stand badly for a time, not knowing why we aren't comfortable, then realize, sometimes too late, that there's a twist or a kink in the body? I know that when I'm not comfortable I won't make a spiritual connection through my knitting. If you need to rest, it's better not to knit. Knitting is not worth pain.

I empty my mind of distractions and stresses of the day. I start knitting to facilitate that effort.

I have an awareness, a feel for the rhythm and sensations of the yarn and needles—coolness, warmth, metal to metal, wood to wood.

After a while my mind starts to listen. This contemplative time has the propensity to sneak up on me. "How can I be more true to myself?" is one question. Listen.

I choose a sense of being worshipful. Acknowledging the existence of the Transcendent leads to the experience of transcendence. Stand with awe at the bigness of God.

That is the center. I aim myself toward the center of the universe.

I love to forget progress. Wow! I have a sock. I love to be surprised. It's part of the mystery. I'm always surprised at how much I like it. Delightful joy comes to me!

Knowing when to stop is a blessing. I stop when it's enough. I don't force it or carry on because I "should." There is no guilt here. I bring what's going on in my heart and mind along throughout the day. Don't compartmentalize. Life is not organized by pigeonholes. Insight comes only by doing. Daily practice—prayer, soul searching, the discipline of holy writings, even work—leads to the deeper levels of our soul and the company of God. What you do is important, but doing it daily is where you find the resting place.

Experiencing the presence of the Divine requires your intention and participation. It's a two-way street, a give and take, a talking and a listening. This takes learning and practice and the realization that each day is new—a new opportunity to walk the spiritual way, a new opportunity for understanding. Newness implies a beginning, and no matter how we've goofed up all our good intentions of the discipline of daily practice in the past, every day is new again and that is a gracious gift. "That we should not wonder if, in the beginning, we often failed in our endeavors, but that at last we should gain a habit, which will naturally produce its acts in us, without our care, and to our exceeding great delight," advised Brother Lawrence in *The Practice of the Presence of God.*

Rituals can give anchors to our beliefs, our faith. They are another form of container. Rituals keep our wheels on the track, reminding us of where we were, where we are, and where we are going. But sometimes ritual becomes the end, not the means. Ritual is not a bad thing, but I think it can take on a life of its own, becoming the religion, not the method. The ritual of daily practice can be a container, but what is important is what is in the box, not the box itself. Being flexible and focusing on the message, the insight, is more important than the ritual. Knitting is not a religion but a container.

The daily practice of our knitting allows for the growth of confidence and creativity. It allows for the growth of patience and usefulness, of peace and rest. Coming daily to our knitting is a place where two friends meet and enjoy each other's company. Holding hands, they walk along laughing and sighing and being together. Come to the daily practice with open expectation (not predetermined expectation) and you will not be disappointed. This goal of open expectation cannot disappoint, for one is always given the gift of the moment.

I'd like to add a comment to Janice's wise advice, especially because she mentions the benefits of reading words of wisdom. Something that rang a bell for me comes from a wonderful book called *Living Simply through the Day: Spiritual Survival in a Complex Age* by Tilden Edwards, published in 1977, which I picked up last year at a library book sale. Tilden writes: "Alan Watts once used a comparison for our moving around. A king and queen are the center of 'where it's at,' so they move with easy, royal bearing. They have no place to 'get.' They have already 'arrived.' Looking deeply at our lineage, we see that we are of the highest royal line: the royal image of God is in us—covered over, but indestructibly there. We need rush nowhere else to get it. We mainly need to attentively relax and dissolve the amnesia that obscures our true identity. Confident evenness in physical movement can provide a regular little jog to our tainted memory. When we know who we really are, life loses false striving and gains simple presence."[6]

Let's just say I'm still striving.

I made a reminder list earlier in my own journey on the Knitting Way that still holds true:

Small actions matter; every action results in a consequence.

Remember to make the small actions.

Small things done in time build.

A mistake is a lesson.

Obstacles and "enemies" are the greatest teachers.

I am not the center of the universe.

I matter.

7
Mind and Body
The Role of Knitting

Like two knitting needles, the sensory system and motor system are made to intertwine, creating a greater sensory awareness of our internal activities and a greater activity of our internal sensory awareness.

—Thomas Hanna, *The Body of Life*

The mind-body connection is one more demonstration of the utter connectedness of everything. The more we discover how our minds and bodies really work, the deeper we're drawn into the mystery beyond the clinical rendition, and the more we can join in and rejoice in the dance of life. Cutting-edge sciences that demonstrate these connections make the headlines, but the oldest and most basic form of mind-body medicine arguably is praying. On the Knitting Way we pray with our hands.

"For humans, the lifelong apprenticeship with the hand begins at birth. We are guided by our hands, and we are indelibly shaped by the knowledge that comes to us through our use of them," writes Frank R. Wilson in *The Hand: How Its Use Shapes the Brain, Language, and Human Culture*. This is appreciated at Waldorf Schools, where knitting is an important part of the curriculum. First-grade students recite a verse before beginning to knit that includes, "My hands are my most useful tools." Educator Bernard Graves in a lecture called "The Craft Gesture" says, "In craft activity Head, Heart and Hands are brought into a particular relationship with each other. Craft activities serve not only to educate in the nature and processes involved with different materials, traditional skills, use of tools and equipment but there is also a more hidden ... therapeutic aspect from which we benefit when practicing true craft. For it is in the very nature of handwork crafts to bring order and to bestow order; to bring order to the materials used and to bestow order upon the maker, the creator. In the practicing of crafts we can indeed rise above our creature state to that of cocreator." Not only does the knitter create the knitting, but the knitter is created by the knitting. The vehicle for this, Graves says, is the "craft gesture" to be seen in the movements of the knitter. "Movements play upon the soul of the human being."[1]

The physical act of knitting has been shown to benefit us by altering our physiology, our mental states, and even our attitudes. There's scientific evidence that knitting synchronizes the right and left sides of the brain, is a conduit to a meditative state, can disrupt the brain's absorption of disturbing images, and can both help develop kinesthetic awareness (a sense of one's body) and improve proprioception ("movement intelligence"). The interpersonal connections forged through knitting can release oxytocin, called the "cuddling" or social attachment hormone. What's more, knitting can bring meaning into existence through hand gestures that act as a kind of "monitor" of the self.

Knitting likely entrains body processes with its soothing rhythm. In entrainment two rhythms interact and synchronize, and there's a tendency for one rhythmic process to adjust to match other rhythms. The naturally occurring rhythms in the body include the heartbeat, breathing, and blood circulation. It has been suggested that all human movements are inherently rhythmic. Some cognitive psychologists contend that perception, attention, and expectation are all rhythmic processes subject to entrainment, and healthy systems require a certain degree of entrainment. According to "In Time with the Music" by Martin

Clayton, Rebecca Sager, and Udo Will, conditions such as autism and Parkinson's disease involve a "disruption of 'normal' entrainment within or between individuals" and autistic people have benefited from entrainment therapy. A gesture by one part of the body tends to entrain gestures by other parts. *Kinesthetic listening,* a kind of crossover sense where performers can feel melodies in their muscles and imagine what it might be like to play what they're hearing, has been reported. This gives new meaning to the music of knitting. In fact, music has been defined as a means by which perception, action, and memory are organized. This definition includes dance, or "eurhythmics," which are gestures guided by music. Musician Mark Nauseef defined dancing in an online article called "Practicing and Making Music ... Without Your Instrument" as "a physical time reference—any repetitive body movement which will clearly mark where we are in the space we are working with." According to that definition, knitting not only has music but also gets you to dance.

Knitting sets a graceful rhythm between the hands and mind. Whatever your knitting style, each hand takes its part, and the brain joins the rhythm. This harmony does the heart good—literally! The regularly bickering right and left sides of the brain have a heart to heart. Chemical transmitters carry the peaceful messages throughout the body and back again to the mind's perceptions and thoughts in a smooth-flowing cycle. When you're fully in a meditative state, your blood pressure drops and your heart rhythm slows. This "integrated healing network, informed by the superintelligence that is the key to life itself, will help us to achieve our greatest potential—if we heed our body's messages," says Bernie S. Siegel, MD, in *Peace, Love and Healing*. He suggests "four to six healing intervals in your day to de-stress yourself." The need for these "healing" intervals, which can be so beautifully tended to with knitting, may be due to our innate "ultradian" rhythm, an internal biological rhythm that repeats in 90- to 120-minute intervals, called the Basic Rest-Activity Cycle, throughout the day and creates REM sleep at night. Chronobiologists tell us that there's a 20-minute "latency" period during each cycle that requires rest. The rest-activity cycle involves alternate shifts in dominance from one side of the brain to another. Overriding the cycle causes stress and can lead to disease. Dr. Herbert Benson, a pioneer in mind-body research who identified the "relaxation response," realized in the 1960s that repetitive activities, like knitting, prompt a physiological shift to a peaceful state.

"Our grandmothers knew all along that our minds and our bodies were connected, even if the scientific community didn't. We've simply provided irrefutable data showing that it's true," says neurobiologist David Felton, head of the Neurobiology and Anatomy Department at the University of Rochester. Felton's research is in psychoneuroimmunology, a field that explores the connection between thoughts and disease. Dr. Felton is speaking of the grandmothers of the past who were connected to the earth and to spirit and *knew* that everything is integrated; everything is connected; and our spirituality affects our bodies, our mental state, and our relationships—and vice versa. Compartmentalization of the different aspects of our lives does us no good. The body, the brain, and the soul are all linked. Each affects the other. Knowing and seeing that there is a physical and spiritual side to everything makes for a fulfilling and healthy life. It shows a respect for yourself as a creation of God—it shows reverence for the Creator. Right and left side, physical and spiritual, emotional and cognitive, we are a whole. Respected sages such as Marion Woodman and Clarissa Pinkola Estés have cited the dishonoring of these primal feminine instincts as the cause of many of the problems we experience in modern living.

A Happy Balance

"The right side of the brain deals with emotion and imagination and the left controls our reasoning. Consequently, if we are upset, the right side of the brain activates the left to provide some balance. This occurs naturally when people knit," says Gavan Naden in an article at www.telegraph.co.uk. Each side of the brain has a different way of "seeing" the world, and these two "personalities" communicate through a connecting "bridge" called the corpus callosum. The more we integrate these sides—right and left—the more harmoniously we function. Knitting fosters this integration. Physically, the bilateral movements of our hands exercise the communication between both sides of the brain. Adding to this "whole brain" effect of knitting is the sensuous input of rhythm, color, and texture combined with mathematical and analytic requirements.

Side-to-side sensations or bilateral stimulation (such as knitting) can help heal emotional distress and remove blocks in thinking, according to practitioners of Eye Movement Desensitization and Reprocessing (EMDR). The FBI, the American Red Cross, and other emergency agencies have found EMDR effective for relieving post-traumatic stress. The EMDR therapist asks the patient to focus on a traumatic memory and a desired resolution. After a course of bilateral stimulation, alternating between the right and left sides of the body, "patients generally think and feel quite differently about the incident, similar incidents, and themselves," according to Edward S. Hume, M.D., in the "Clinical Wisdom" section of his website, www.pshrink.com. He goes on to describe the left side of the brain *that controls the right side of the body* as "more positive in outlook, more analytical, looking ahead" and the right side of the brain tending toward "a more morose outlook, more holistic, scanning the world for threats.... I suspect that the alternate-side stimulation occurring in EMDR might be simultaneously stimulating positive networks in the left brain while invoking negative networks in the right brain." EMDR has been described as an entrainment procedure. Psychologist Dr. Emily Holmes did experiments showing that bilateral stimulation can disrupt the brain's absorption of disturbing images that could return as flashbacks.

Feeling comfortable with the physical process is a problem for new knitters. It's an awkward time, a time when some get frustrated and discouraged. There are so many possible ways to knit. Perseverance is called for. You need to do it until you discover what works for you and get into the rhythm. You can only discover this for yourself through experience. Isn't that like life in general? Janice says, "Don't be bound or bamboozled by other people's solutions and prescriptions."

Here are the knitting styles among four friends:

I knit continental style, holding the yarn with my left forefinger, and just move my wrists.

Janice doesn't move her wrists; she moves from her shoulders and wraps with the right hand. She says she won't persevere with a nonintuitive technique.

Gway-Yuang (Karen) Ko uses the method recommended in *The Principles of Knitting*, which she learned in Taiwan, a pencil hold, wrapping with the index finger of her right hand.

Sharyn's right hand barely moves. She tucks the needle under her right arm and wraps with her right finger and knits with a fluid motion.

Once knitting skills are learned, lower levels of the brain (the cerebellum and basal ganglia of the brain stem) can take over from the cortex, the gray matter where most higher-level brain function takes place. This is what's meant by "knitting on autopilot." Writer Anthony Burgess referred to this phenomenon in a 1974 interview. He said, "What am I working at here? I'm writing a symphony at the moment here, but a symphony to me is rather like a woman knitting, it keeps one part of my brain occupied while another part can concentrate on new literary ventures."

Once movements are memorized and "in the muscle," they can be accomplished without looking. That's why we don't have to remember or relearn our hand movements in knitting. Once learned, our hands and fingers do the remembering. (We *are* "fearfully and wonderfully made.") Then proprioception—a sense of where each part of the body is and how it's moving, another form of awareness— takes over. Proprioceptors are sense organs found within joints and muscles that unconsciously tell us where we are in relation to our environment. It's interesting that, according to Neil Douglas-Klotz in "The Natural Breath," "The Kabbalah, a Jewish mystical work, teaches that without Holy Wisdom *(hokhmah)* or 'witnessing awareness' ... ultimately tied up with the body's proprioceptive awareness, the subconscious self (*nephesh* in Hebrew) splits into a multiplicity of discordant voices forgetful of the divine Unity."[2]

We can knit without this body awareness, but the knitting will be mechanical, restricted, and constricted rather than open, interactive, and creative—a hindrance to accessing the spiritual. In other words, for change to occur, sensory feedback is vital. The body needs to know itself in order to transform fixed patterns—and so does the soul. A person's idiosyncrasies in moving are as individual as a fingerprint. Police use this phenomenon to identify disguised suspects in surveillance films. "Even when we think we are choosing an action deliberately, the manner in which we do it is the sum of our history," writes body psychotherapist Roz Caroll in an article on her website www.thinkbody.co.uk.

Regaining Balance in Life and Knitting

When I knit too long and my body hurts, it's a danger signal, like a car's oil depletion indicator, descriptively known as the "idiot light," that screams for attention because I haven't been aware and taken care of its needs.

With awareness I will stop or change something, and adapt to keep myself in a place of balance and health. On the Knitting Way, as I learn to focus attention on the present moment, I will consider: How do I feel now? What is my body telling me? How do I feel alive? Is my body aligned? I'll shift positions, hold the needles lightly, learn what is comfortable and what's a strain, do neck rolls, shoulder circles, ankle rolls, and long back stretches. Do tai chi, get up and dance, go for a walk, and leave the knitting home for a while! That's what makes sense and what's best because that's how our bodies are made. That's what our earthy grandma would tell us.

The Arthritis Victoria Organization for Musculo-Skeletal Health in Australia puts it another way: "Move It or Lose It." They remind us to take a PAUSE anytime we've been sitting for more than an hour by remembering this acrostic:

Posture: Slumping can become permanent unless you move your body in the opposite direction.

Attitude: Taking a short break enables you to return with a fresh approach.

Unwind: Physical and mental stress accumulates without your being aware of it.

Stretch: Muscles and joints need to be stretched.

Energize: Breathe and move to improve circulation.[3]

"Cumulative-trauma disorders," such as painful carpal tunnel syndrome, can be prevented. How? Don't subject yourself to cumulative trauma! If you are knitting for long periods, listen to your body, follow the PAUSE imperatives and do the following exercises before knitting, recommended by a team of orthopedic surgeons, even before starting again after a break:

Extend and stretch both arms and wrists in front of you as if they're in a handstand position. Hold for five seconds.

Straighten both wrists and relax your fingers.

Make a tight fist with both hands.

Bend both wrists down while keeping the fist. Hold for five seconds.

Straighten both wrists and relax fingers. Hold for five seconds.

Repeat these steps ten times.

Paul J. Sorgi, MD, a clinical instructor in psychiatry at Harvard Medical School, in an article titled "Regaining Balance in Your Life" at www.bottomlinesecrets.com, includes steps that seem to invite the Knitting Way. Dr. Sorgi suggests that we need to have downtime in the evening with several hours of soft light and quiet activity, and advises that we avoid TV and the Internet for two hours before bedtime. In addition to vigorous activity thirty minutes at least three times a week, Dr. Sorgi says that we need rhythmic motion—movement that has a pattern and flow to it—which has been shown to reduce nervous tension. Dr. Sorgi prescribes walking whenever we can, rocking in a rocking chair twice a day for at least fifteen minutes, and "for every four hours of inactivity, spend fifteen minutes knitting, writing by hand, or drawing." He further advises us to avoid "superficial contact" for a half-hour every day—to, in our words, seek the authentic and the real, a reminder that the opposite of the superficial is the Holy. And he tells us to find groups of like-minded people to share our energy with.

To be whole, healthy, and fully alive, writer James Harvey Stout advocated what he called the "Grandma Principle" for "a balance between our human perspective and the transcendental." He wrote, "We are 'humans' not 'souls' ... We can freely choose the perspective which is most appropriate, effective, and loving for our purpose in this moment. If our purpose is to balance ourselves, we can select the human viewpoint without worrying that we are sacrificing our 'spirituality'; in fact, we can appreciate this opportunity to explore spirit as it expresses itself in the human world and the physical world." In our opinion, Grandma is a sponsor of the Knitting Way.

Space between the Loops
Knitting for Weight Control?

How many calories do we burn when we knit? A chart giving calories expended in different activities (calories per hour for each kilogram of weight, which I converted to pounds) indicates 0.3175 calories per pound, per hour. So the currently 150-pound me (Linda), according to the chart, works off about 48 calories when I knit, the same number I use in dressing and undressing and almost twice as many as when sewing or writing. Wow! An hour of knitting will burn off about four saltines. However, as we know, there's knitting and then there's knitting! I suspect whoever put together the chart was considering basic stockinette at a relaxed pace. The same chart had gradations for piano playing, ranging from the basic 0.36 calories burned per pound per hour to 0.64 for Beethoven's *Appassionata* (perhaps knitting a lace shawl?), with a further upgrade to 0.9 for Liszt's *Tarantella* (an Aran coat?), which would work off about 135 calories for me.

Bearing Witness
Following Your Own Knitting to Find Your Story

I was struggling with this chapter when I attended a lecture by Holocaust historian Yehuda Bauer, who says that we need to commit ourselves to three additions to the Ten Commandments. These are: "Thou shall not be a perpetrator; thou shall not be a victim; and thou shall never, but never, be a bystander." This prescription went right to the heart of bearing witness. Although Bauer is speaking to the potential for genocide inherent in our humanness, each of us always has the ability and responsibility to *choose* not to be a victim, a perpetrator, or a bystander. We are never victims once we recognize that no one else can control our attitudes or our behaviors. These are freedoms that can't be taken away. And we need to recognize that we are all capable of being perpetrators. Being aware makes all the difference. On the path we find how intrinsically we're all connected. What you do affects me and what I do affects you. As bystanders, who feel uninvolved with what happens, we're out of touch with the reality of our lives. For meaning, for transformation and transcendence, for peace of mind and peace in the world, all the wisdom traditions tell us that we must bear witness to the truth in our own lives beginning with and beyond our own stories. On the Knitting Way we begin to bear witness through telling and listening to our knitting stories. It is a journey where we discover that, although our conscious egos seem to be the center of our personalities, they are not the center of our whole beings.

What do you really *hate* in someone else? The wisdom traditions and behavioral sciences tell us that what we hate most is the part of ourselves we've disowned as "not us" and have projected onto the "other." We all have an unconscious shadow side where the conscious ego-self has stashed everything too painful and frightening to confront. We may *hate* another knitter's "pushiness" in getting her designs published, but secretly desire to push there ourselves. In our subterranean depths resides what Clarissa Pinkola Estés in *Women Who Run with the Wolves* calls the "river beneath the river," where we touch the mystery of "The One Who Knows." It's where our real desires, energy, and powers are, and where we must look if we're truly on a spiritual journey. To bear witness to our whole self, which includes what's conscious and what's in shadow behind the sanitized "mask" we show the world, takes all the courage, care, and attention that we've been cultivating on the Knitting Way. When we feel cut off from our own depths, rather than connecting with our sacred places, we may be tempted to rush to fill the empty feeling behind the mask with something that literally "occupies" us from outside. I know I do.

Here's where the TV really shines. It's just the ticket for blocking our own thoughts, as we use its noise and images to occupy ourselves. But Fred Rogers, creator of *Mr. Rogers' Neighborhood* for children's television, considered the space between the television set and the viewer as "holy ground" where he tried to provide an alternative to the "bombardment" that was on TV. He ended each show with the message we all need to hear, "You've made this day special by just you're being you. You know, there's just one person in the whole world like you, and people can like you exactly as you are," adding, as the show evolved, "and you can like them exactly as they are." "That completes the circle," Rogers was reported as saying in an article at www.Newsweek.com. "It seems like a subtle shift, but if a child realizes that he or she can be loved as he or she is, their neighbor can be, too.... I want to know kids have choices in expressing how they feel.... I want to show them a whole lot of ways to express who they are and how they feel." Mr. Rogers's words moved me when he came to TV and I had children of my own. I still get all teary as I type them. I wonder if I'm the only one.

Are You Knitting on Empty?

Many of us don't like ourselves exactly as we are. We don't give ourselves a chance to face and feel our genuine preferences, desires, demons, fears, and sorrows, and we're too afraid to imagine there's something beyond us that we can't control. We cover up the parts of ourselves we can't accept, or project them onto someone else. We feel worried, anxious, righteous, insecure, out of control, angry, depressed, jealous, guilty, and ashamed. Our motives become complicated. We may knit to win love, show off, comply, placate, compete, fill our time, prove ourselves, or even to self-medicate. Social scientists have identified a continuum of behaviors, from healthy patterns to self-medicating dependencies, that can help us bear witness in our knitting: *Patterns* help organize our lives, such as "I like to knit in the morning." *Habits* are more specific and idiosyncratic than patterns—"I always knit when I wake up." *Compulsions* are an attempt to relieve tensions caused by inner feelings we want to avoid or control, as in "I must have my knitting along to relax." And *addictions* are compulsions that have progressed to dysfunction and rigidity. By the compulsion level, the reward is not from the knitting itself, but from the reduction or release of tension. Knitting, at this level of dependence, could interfere with daily living and have harmful consequences.

To gauge where your knitting lies on the dependency continuum, answer the following questions:

Do you knit when you need to do something else?

Do you binge on knitting and yarn shopping?

Have you run out of room for your yarn stash?

Do you feel pain after over-knitting?

Is your knitting negatively affecting the way you live your life?

Do you knit to escape from worries or trouble?

Have you ever been treated for a condition physically related to knitting?

Does your knitting behavior make you or others unhappy?

Are you chronically dissatisfied with your knitting?

Do you keep knitting when you want to stop?

If any of these questions resonate with you, recognize that you may be in a negative loop. In other words, you may be indulging in empty-calorie knitting rather than knitting that nourishes you. Being willing to observe yourself honestly is the first step in caring for your soul. In the process of self-discovery, as Thomas Moore said in *Care of the Soul,* you account for all your "sheep" and watch "whatever is wandering and grazing—the latest addiction ... or a troubling mood.... You take back what has been *disowned....* Soul is not a thing but a dimension of experiencing life and ourselves that has to do with depth, value, relatedness, heart and personal substance.... Befriend the problem." Moore also talks about "primordial femininity" and advises us to "become acquainted with ancient and profound roots of womanhood and discover how to truly nourish yourself."[1] That's what our journey together is all about.

It's the Story We All Share

We're all imperfect. It is the story we all share. The founders of Alcoholics Anonymous rediscovered the ancient wisdom of the Spirituality of Imperfection, which is concerned with the truth of being human. The Spirituality of Imperfection recognizes that in denying our flaws and our errors, we deny ourselves. Spiritual discoveries, the founders said, "cannot be made for us, or for anyone else, by someone else. Nor are they ever found once and for all. Each day requires constant rediscovery and continually new insight into what it means to be human, what it means to exist as a fully human being ... and that spirituality involves not magic's manipulation, but the wonder inherent in mystery."[2] The 12 Steps help us move from fear to trust, from self-pity to gratitude, from resentment to acceptance, and from dishonesty to honesty.

A Knitter's 12-Step Program

1. Face that I can't solve or control everything. Give up my "stuckness." I'm not God. *Seeing all my yarn swept away in a tornado would be a quick lesson.*
2. Create a space for solutions to come to me rather than demand that things always work out the way I want them to. *That's how I get to Aha!*
3. Trust life. Pay attention. Live and let live. I'm human and I have choices! *I'm free to knit in the ways my heart leads.*
4. Make a fearless self-inventory. Blaming someone else focuses attention outside instead of on myself. Be who I am, not who I want to be. Remove judgment to avoid blame and shame. *I secretly enjoyed hearing about the messy ends at the back of Kaffe Fassett's sweater because I fear my own knitting reveals my inner messiness.*
5. Admit my mistakes honestly to myself, God, and one other person. Now, as I recognize I'm not a bystander in my life, I take responsibility for my behavior. *I don't have to be ashamed of being human.*
6. Be willing to give up the defenses that keep me stuck and accept caring. *I can ask for help to find a better way.*
7. Pray, when I realize I want something beyond my control. This lets me want what I want even

though there's a risk of being disappointed. *God, help me to express and spread love through my knitting.*

8. Make a list of people I've harmed and be willing to make amends. Saying, "I chose to" instead of "I had to," and "I won't" instead of "I can't" is the difference between accepting the responsibility of free will and playing the role of a victim. Reclaim power over what I can control—my choice. Focus on being happy rather than "right." *I realize that knitting the cashmere baby sweaters when the twins were born, which became Barbie coats when they emerged from the washer and dryer, did not take the new mother's needs into consideration.*

9. Actually make amends.

10. Continue to take a personal inventory. Stay aware. *Did opening that post office box, to secretly receive my yarn from Patternworks so my husband wouldn't find out, bring me closer to where I want to go?*

11. Make a daily practice to contact the Source of Life. This reminds me that everything I need is already here and prepares me for the "next right thing." *That's what I'm doing on the Knitting Way.* C. S. Lewis said, "Believe in God and you will have to face hours when it seems obvious that this material world is the only reality; disbelieve in Him and you must face hours when this material world seems to shout at you that it is not all. No conviction, religious or irreligious, will, of itself, end once and for all [these doubts] in the soul. Only the practice of Faith resulting in the habit of Faith will gradually do that."[3]

12. As I awaken to a new way of experiencing the world, I carry the message to others. It's reflected in everything I do. *I bring it to my knitting group, which brings it to the larger community.*

Has There Really Been Love in Every Stitch?

"Hidden things hinder wholeheartedness," observed Cassian, known as the Father of Western monasticism.

When we look at my Project Selection Mind Map, the potential for things to go wrong seems to be overwhelming. You could wonder how any of us knit at all with this vast opportunity to go astray. Our own hidden motivations increase this potential. Knitting patterns can have errors, but more often our problems stem from our own inexperience or from misinterpretations, prejudices, dogmas, and impatience—our own stories. Janice's "My Knitting" chart (on pages 172–173) shows some scenarios we might recognize. In the words of the cartoon character Pogo, "We have met the enemy and he is us."

The Project Selection Mind Map: A knitter's maze of possibilities.

Ask yourself whether you're taking responsibility for your results and your feelings or you're placing blame. You are responsible for the whole project. It is *your* creation. If it doesn't fit what you think you wanted, look a little closer. Ask: "What am I not seeing?" "Who is knitting?" "Who am I knitting for?"

The same Mind Map also shows the potential for things to go right. Through this viewpoint a sea of possibilities opens up, providing opportunities for growth where we can discover and create what, in Kristin Nicholas's words, "suits" ourselves. First, we need to find out what "suiting ourselves" is. Sometimes we've locked ourselves in a limited point of view, which writer Jeffrey Eugenides articulated in a *New York Times* article about the Tour de France, headlined "Summer, from the Inside": "Those kids were having a real summer. Had I had a real summer when I was their age? It seemed to me I hadn't. As a teenager I had been in a room similar to this, or perhaps the room I remembered was not a real room but only my personality, the viewing booth from which I look out on life. But that's how I feel about summer. Summer always happens to other people." That sounds familiar to me. But now I recognize it's a viewing booth that I can leave. To let go of the feeling of lack, look at it, hold it open, and allow something else to emerge. It's scary but it's the only way to soar.

Janice is experienced in selecting projects that work for her. She says: "I am currently making cozy slippers for the grandchildren. Little Ryan's are a dark, heathery blue and very grown up, manly looking. Isabella's are a dusty pink and, sure, they would be adorable with little embroidered flowers or other girlie embellishments added, but I'm not doing it. Isabella will just get the little yarns and threads caught on things, causing snags and holes. So they shall remain as plain as her brother's. It's question of sanity. It's more important to me to have a finished item being used than a finished item that will be praised for its charm and prettiness. I won't make myself crazy. A two-year-old won't care. 'Some are fancy on the outside, some are fancy on the inside,' Mr. Rogers would say. These slippers will be fancy on the inside, as they will contain the sweet toes of a little girl. This approach proves a sensible one. Finding a sensible way appeals to me." Can you understand why I value Janice's counsel?

Many of my memorable projects did not turn out as I had hoped, although I didn't have any idea of how to listen to what they had to tell me at the time. My all-time awful project was a bulky sweater with the picture of a horse head on the back that was commissioned by a neighbor BP (Before Patternworks). The process and product

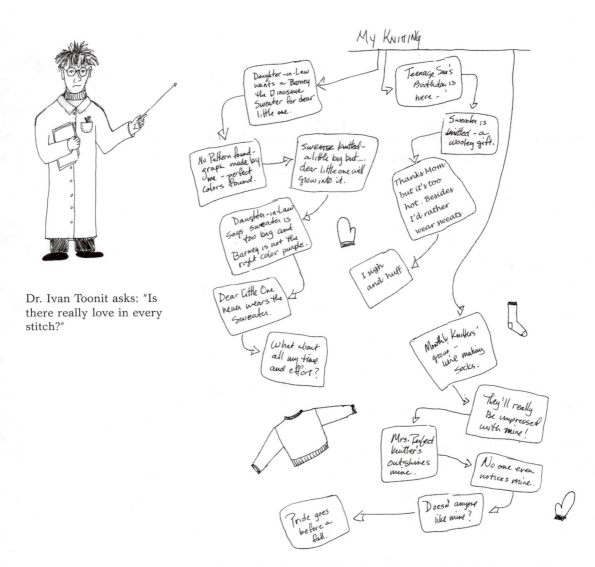

Dr. Ivan Toonit asks: "Is there really love in every stitch?"

made me feel more like the other end of the horse. I have blocked out my neighbor's reception of it. My practice on the Knitting Way continues to reveal the difference between knitting from the heart and knitting for all the wrong reasons.

When I was a young mother, my mother-in-law and I each knitted lace dresses from the same pattern that we

Neighbor's daughter having a baby.

Beautiful Lace Tablecloth Started for Mother-in-law.

The Joy is in the knitting

It's a girl! Perfect lace patterned sweater created.

When projects are complete

cut the yarn

Set them free

Washing Instructions not followed.

It takes a long time.

Let them go

Baby's Teddy Bear now wears the sweater.

She loves it But....

The "Baby Birds" have left the nest.

At least the Teddy Bear loves me.

It's secreted away in a drawer.

Don't Bring them back in.

"I don't want anything to happen to it," She says.

It never sees the light of day.

Move on to a new joy.

"What was the point?" I say.

got from a loopy discount yarn store in the far reaches of Brooklyn, which had the finest yarns tumbling from piles that reached the ceiling. Mine was in burgundy. I can see it now. I thought it looked beautiful until I saw hers. My knitting was loose, with big, lacy holes, while hers sharply defined the pattern stitch. To maintain decency I needed to dye a slip to match. I wish I had a picture of it on me.

I can only imagine. My dear mother-in-law lived in the next apartment building, but I seem to have knit it in a vacuum. I missed making that connection.

In recent years, I've erred on the side of too tight and too small. The first thing I knit for Alex, my first grandbaby-to-be, was Cottage Creations's Babies and Bears sweater. I wanted it to be perfect and it wound up sized for a doll. Years later I performed surgery on the hood to accommodate the ears of granddaughter Amanda's bear. Another painful result was my beautiful Hanne Falkenberg jacket, the knitting of which got me through my father's final sickness in 1999. It came out tighter, less "flowing," and smaller than the model I saw Hanne herself wearing that had inspired me to knit it. A repeat of the same error! I'm convinced that our myths determine gauge more than a gauge swatch. You really do see (and measure) what you believe! I had implanted the myth that I knit too loosely (translated in my mind as imperfectly). I believe I was trying to be perfect.

I designed a Chanel-style sweater in 2001 that had a pleasing two-color pattern stitch. I loved knitting the fabric but had some fit and design difficulties. I became locked in a battle with it. I wasn't letting all those hours and plans go to waste! I wound up finishing it, and I even wear it occasionally, but the fight shows. The Yiddish word for this sweater is *ongepotchket*, or excessively and unaesthetically decorated. The "one more thing" added that ruins a project. I couldn't accept that it wasn't working and kept covering up. I now recognize that pride and shame fueled a lot of my knitting.

Another example of learning to listen to your knitting projects is a knit-from-the-top-down sweater for my husband Marvin with a very dark, almost black-blue yarn and a pleasing-to-knit (when in the right mental frame) corrugated pattern stitch that I started on a tension-ridden trip. The sweater and I were plagued with mistakes that I would find inches later. I finally decided on a new plan.

I used the yarn for a wonderful kimono-style sweater, Thai from *Simply Knit*—for myself! I knit the border band in Koigu, in a mesmerizing 3–3 diagonal rib. I just need to finish a sleeve. I'll show you how it turns out at our website www.theknittingway.com. I see the last incident as progress on the path. I could admit that what I was knitting was not working, and I was able to change gears and knit a sweater for myself—in all senses.

What can be learned from these stories?

Creating Safe Spaces to Hear Our Stories

When I was trying to sort this out, I noticed in my book pile *The Sacred Art of Listening* by Kay Lindahl, the founder of The Listening Center, a breath-giving book hidden from me in plain sight for over a year, since July 20, 2003, the date printed on the receipt that I found inside. I recommend that you get a copy of the book, in which every word and image leads to deeper understanding of what the sacred art of listening is. Lindahl tells us that to practice the Sacred Art of Listening we need to listen for new possibilities and ask, "'What just happened?' ... 'What did I learn from that?' ... 'How did I grow from that?' ... 'What's next for me?' ... 'How did this impact others in my life?' ... 'How does it relate to patterns in my past?'" She advises that we need to pose questions to create openings, "What would it be like if ... ?" And, we need to shift our attention from trying to "fix" things by asking, "What is it that, if it were present, would lead to what we want?' Look for what is possible, not just what is wrong.... Creating something that didn't exist before cannot happen without change.... Too often I am back into old patterns, something is unresolved in my past, I am carrying my past with me into the future."[4]

Lindahl writes that the "promise" of her book is that "you can learn to listen from the essence of your being by taking a few minutes a day for quiet time with your authentic self.... I recommend a daily contemplative practice of some kind to everyone I counsel. I would go so far as to say that it is an essential practice for the sacred art of listening ... to discern what really matters and let go of what does not, [be] less likely to judge other people, accept our own basic goodness, cultivate an open mind, transform our motivations and purify our intentions, achieve inner freedom to serve truthfully in the outer world.... Find a practice that works for you and make a commitment to it. Practice for at least thirty consecutive days. Your life will be transformed by an increased awareness of God's presence and a deepening sense of gratitude and appreciation. Your ability to listen deeply to yourself and to others will never be the same." To us knitting enthusiasts, this seems to be recommending the Knitting Way.

As things happen, it turned out that Maura Shaw, the editor of *The Knitting Way,* was also the editor of *The Sacred Art of Listening,* and Maura encouraged me to correspond with Kay Lindahl by e-mail. Kay wrote back that her mother had taught her to knit when she was about nine years old and she knit a lot for several years, but cut back after having children. In the past few years she says she has "taken it up again—with a vengeance," and confided, "Knitting often calms me down and gets me to be more centered, especially in the midst of chaos, internal or external. There's something very satisfying about working with my hands and producing something. Most results of my work are intangible and it's wonderful to actually see a finished product!"

At the same time that I'm learning to view my mistakes as openings to something deeper, I'm finding that I'm better able to be willing to forgive, even myself. Judy Allen, a follower of *A Course in Miracles* in Portland, Oregon, described a way to look at forgiveness through the lens of knitting in her Web article, "Unraveling the Past." "When a miracle (defined as a change of mind) occurs, time and space don't follow the rules.... Since it is an out-of-pattern time interval, the ordinary considerations of time and space do not apply.... [Think of] forgiveness, as a miracle— a change of mind—that undoes or unravels the effects of the mistake of deciding that we had been hurt." After unraveling while praying, "All the effects of my mistake, all my pain and misery and anger were erased, obliterated, gone as if they had never existed. I was restored to truth, restored to a state where I could begin again, choosing differently this time. And I could now create a different reality. Time was yarn rewound back onto the ball—now I could re-knit, with a different outcome."[5]

Space between the Loops

Letting Go

I've always had a sense of success about my knitting, although I definitely made mistakes. For a long while I kept them to help me remember that, in a process, you don't arrive at knowledge without some bumps and potholes. That is the way life is. That is the way the spiritual life is.

In the nonspiritual world, success is measured by how beautiful your knitting is. It's measured by your skill as a knitter, by your level of involvement in the craft, by whether you've been published in a magazine or written a book about knitting, even by how many knitting buddies you have. Being successful means something very different in the spiritual world. As Michael Yaconelli wrote in *Messy Spirituality*, "The spiritual life is not a life of success; it is a life of faithfulness, and it is not easy."

Being spiritually successful is measured by where you went and Who went with you. It's about how you experienced the presence of the Beautifully Divine Being. It's not about how many candles you lit, or the striving after the warm glowing feeling of serenity. It's not about feelings or the "altar" that you set up. All those things can focus your attention but they are not where the spiritual lies. It lies in your heart. It's learning something about yourself and being transformed. It lies in your faith.

Sometimes faith is hard. Being spiritual is very often dirty business. It's measured by how well you hold on and Who you hold onto when life is hard. It's easy to be spiritual when you're sitting in your cozy knitting chair with the music playing and the cat at your feet. It's hard to be spiritual when you have only $6 to buy food for the week. It's hard to be spiritual when the car breaks down again and you have more bills than money. It's hard to be spiritual when your closest friends move far away. It's hard to be spiritual when you miscarry your very wanted second child. It's hard to be spiritual when your baby child is on his deathbed. But your need to be spiritual is at its highest during those times.

In 1985 I gave birth to my fourth son, Evan. He was a failure-to-thrive baby and after many attempts to find his malady, he was finally diagnosed with biliary atresia, a fatal disease that destroys the bile ducts and causes cirrhosis of the liver. By the time he was diagnosed, at the age of six months, his liver was almost completely gone. The only "cure" is a liver transplant. No guarantees. Evan was placed on the National Transplantation List to wait for a donor liver. We embarked on a regime of megadoses of vitamins and nutrients. You need your liver to metabolize many nutrients. Evan couldn't do it. We had to keep him as strong as possible until the transplant could be done. In June of 1986, when Evan was eight months old, a liver was found. Baby and I jumped in a chartered plane and flew to Boston for the transplant to be done at Massachusetts General Hospital. On the way out the door to go to the airport I couldn't find my knitting. I remember being very upset about getting to Boston and not having my knitting to fall into. I had to go without it. My husband, Gene, was able to find it and he brought it with him on the four-hour drive to Boston.

The surgery lasted about ten hours through the night. I couldn't knit. The surgeon came to us after the surgery and explained that the prognosis was very "grim." There was something wrong with the new liver. She said Evan would be re-listed for another liver. They would do everything to keep him alive until a new one could be acquired. She suggested we make funeral arrangements. I couldn't knit. Only strength from God could sustain me.

Evan lived for another week with virtually no liver function. Then, a miracle—a new liver was found. Another transplant surgery, and liver number two seemed to be working. For one week we witnessed a dramatic change in our child. He actually looked the healthiest he had ever looked, even with all the tubes and machines. We were very hopeful, but I still couldn't knit, even though I had my project with me. Then at dinnertime a call came to the home of our friends with whom we were staying in Boston. "You need to get to the hospital as soon as you can," said the voice on the phone. When we arrived at Evan's room, the doctors and nurses were administering CPR on his tiny little body—he only weighed twelve pounds. They talked about cutting him open again and doing something radical to save his life. We said, "No more surgery. Let him go." That's about as spiritual as it gets, when you say "Take my child, God." It took a while, but the knitting did come back, and with a force. Sometimes going through the wilderness brings clarity and a heightened creativity. Passing through the curtain of despair into hope and life is a gift.

We have to let go of any hate, anger, or an unforgiving spirit. These things only imprison the carrier. Sometimes it's hard to do this, but this is the most important thing that you can do, maybe even must do, in order to dwell in your spiritual self. I don't have words to tell anyone how to do this. Hurt and pain are hard to let go of. I can tell you it takes time. I can tell you it takes a belief that there is Someone bigger in control. It requires a leap of faith, a leap of trust, even if you don't understand or know what or Who to trust in. I know that without God's hand on me, and my faith in that, I might still be gripped by the grief of loss.

179

To rest in faith is a decision. It has been nineteen years since the death of my infant son. Grief and despair can overwhelm and strength is gone, absolutely gone during bereavement. Maybe you're even angry with God. I think God can handle that. These are natural emotions and progressions of emotions, but holding on, re-living, keeping these emotions fueled will cause you to miss the good things that will come to your life, and they will come. Own your emotions, then let them go. Prolonged grief is a cage. The betrayal of a loved one or a friend, hurt, and rejection held onto—all are cages. Anger likes to fuel itself. Bitterness and unforgiveness feed each other. Keeping the flames of these emotions fanned will wholly (not holy) interfere with any listening or learning to be done on your part and will only lead to bitterness and closing of your soul and a missing out on life. Forgiveness is for your sake. Holding on is imprisonment. Letting go is freedom. As Ursula Le Guin said, "Love doesn't just sit there, like a stone, it has to be made like bread, remade all the time, made new."

Building Community

We all yearn for love and connection. Within our knitting group, we can create a community—an atmosphere of acceptance where all members experience connection. In the community, a safe space, we're free to be what and who we are. Community doesn't happen if we see others and ourselves as needing "fixing." We don't need to be controlled, but our stories need to be witnessed. When we accept ourselves, we can bear witness for one another. Our stories determine how we live. When we discover and own the stories we're living by, we can expand and transform them from our souls. Honoring all our stories is an essential part of a spiritual path. It's vital in raising healthy children and building relationships. Psychologist Dr. Michael Brody pointed to a disturbing trend in toys in a *New York Times* article titled "Why Smart Toys Aren't

Always So Smart." He said that some new toys are so highly structured that "they superimpose someone else's story on the kids." We can help counteract this trend with needles, yarn, and love.

Space between the Loops
Going with the Flow

The Knitting Way is a meandering river quietly flowing along, allowing the little streams and estuaries to branch off on their own for a time, then calling them back to join the mother flow, the continuation of the journey. It wanders along, growing wide in some places, then becoming narrow again in others. We all have times when our knitting is unstoppable and other times when we barely touch the needles. We knit or don't knit to the ebb and flow of our spirit. We all have times when we knit alone and times when we join the connective spirit of the group.

One of the most lovely and satisfying times of my life was when I worked as a volunteer cook for a summer camp. It was hard work, constantly, from pre-dawn to well after dusk. Our kitchen crew was made up mostly of women (husband o' mine was also part of the team—a rooster among the hens), and what a joy to be working, physically working, with other women. We sang and laughed, cried and bore frustrations together over the work of our hands. I have noticed that this cuts across cultures and times. From women taking their laundry to the river rocks, to the grinding of grain, the planting of seeds in the fields, the drawing of water, the baking of bread at the village oven, the quilting bees, the sewing circles, and the ladies' auxiliary—all these activities and many others are marked over the centuries as times of women joining together to complete a common task. Joined together in common work is such a pleasing and fulfilling and happy way to work. These are times of connection, times of getting to know and understand and reveal. Work is rhythm and rhythm is opening. Just as the alone times in knitting are fulfilling, pleasing, and connecting, so are the group knitting experiences. Knitters gathered together and all using their hands at the same time is joy. Connection just happens: you don't have to force it.

According to Janice, community springs from the commonality of the members. It can be diverse or homogenous, restful or radical, and all at the same time. It is made up of human beings who are all those things, sometimes all at the same time. It rests on the human beings and happens when two or more come together, drawn by the force that each one shares with the other. Knitters instantly sense this force in one another. Groups form and the personality of each group is different because the people it contains are different. Some groups exist to knit for charity, some for making political statements, some for the opportunity to just have the discipline of getting projects done. There can be impediments to community. Some bring agendas filled with personal neediness. For some, it's all about "me." The community is about the community as *the whole*, not me as *the individual*. Some groups have evolved to a place where the soul of each knitter is connected to the other. True community happens when people are allowed to be who and what they are. The leaders of such groups understand their role as facilitator, not ruler. Lifetime bonds form in such groups. Each member of a community is important to the whole.

Sacred depth, honest awareness, love, safety, and space for our stories and communities can all be found in the knitting. Our knitting witnesses and testifies to who we are. Wisdom learned from experience one day adds to the wisdom of the next day, and we never stop adding if we are seeking and open, and honest and willing. Come with us as we explore being part of the community of knitting and passing on the knitting and the wisdom.

Paying It Forward
Passing On the Knitting and the Wisdom

On Being a Knitting Mentor

"The gulf that separates those who knit and those who don't is only a few hours, or a few pages. But, to cross it, you need to know that you can. You need a knitter," writes Elaine Rowley, the original publisher and editor of *Knitter's Magazine* in the foreword to Elizabeth Zimmermann's *Knitting Around*. "I knit today because of Elizabeth," she goes on. "Had I not found her perhaps I would have bumped into some other knee, but then again … a knitter, a yarn shop, a magazine, a family, might not have been."

Think of the power you have in your hands! You could be that knitter who bridges the gulf. Who knows what will come of it when you teach someone to knit—a new way of thinking, peace of mind, a masterpiece, a new career (for both of you), friendship, love—quite a responsibility. But Joseph Campbell distinguished an ordinary teacher from a mentor. He said, "The teacher just gives you information, generally without a clue about the difference between it and wisdom…. The mentor is the one who helps you find your own way."[1] Opportunities to become a mentor will cross your knitting path as you find your own way.

Janice notes, "Be generous in your mentoring. Understand that there are many who have stories of the teacher/mentor who 'ruined' it for them. Have you

experienced, possibly, a teacher who killed the beginning
fire of enthusiasm that burned in you? A generous mentor
fans the flames. Allow the student to lead. A mentor is a
servant. The needs, abilities, interests, and passions of the
student guide a mentor—anything less than that and
teachers are burning the coals of their own worth. Bring
your best and most generous enthusiasm for your knitting
to impart to your student."

Tried and True Tips for Introducing Kids (or Anyone) to Knitting

You can use these nine steps with anyone who has the
enthusiasm and openness of a child.

1. *Pre-Knitting:* Allow the student, who doesn't have
   previous yarn experience, to grasp the idea of the
   knit stitch by showing how to finger knit. Begin
   with a slip stitch over the index finger. *Yarn over
   finger and pull loop over yarn-over. Repeat from *
   to form chain. This is a great way to get the feel
   and understanding of the dynamics of the loop.
   It's a privilege and a thrill to witness the wonder
   of discovery as your student "gets" it.
   Kids may like to use the chain as a necklace,
   bracelet, strap for a purse (to be knitted), or just to
   meander around the room! It's a great activity for
   a long car trip.
2. *Have a piece of knitting prepared for the student:*
   Cast on 10–20 stitches and knit for 1 inch in a
   light color worsted weight yarn (so it's easy to see
   the stitches) on short (more manageable) US 8 or
   US 10 needles. We've found it easier to teach (and
   learn) how to knit than how to cast on.
3. *Show the student how to accomplish a knit stitch:*
   Allow the student to begin knitting on the swatch
   and find a comfortable style. One memory rhyme
   goes: "Into the front door, yarn around the back.

Out through the window, off jumps Jack." It's a great help for carrying through the concept.

4. *After learning the knit stitch, the student naturally progresses to the "knit on" cast-on:* *Knit into the stitch without removing it from the needle and place the new loop back on the left-hand needle. A new stitch has been cast on. Repeat from *.

5. *First Project Ideas:* The knitted piece, depending on size and shape, can be formed into:

A small purse (by folding and sewing sides and adding button loop to flap);

A snake or a worm (by gathering top, bottom, and neck, then sewing seam and stuffing with yarn scraps, fleece, or fiberfill);

A ball (from a square by gathering top and bottom and sewing side seam and stuffing.

An animal (the pattern for making a bunny out of a 6-inch square of knitting can be found at www.heartstringsfiberarts.com, at the bottom in the section of free patterns called "HeartStrings' Gift to You"); or

Anything that bubbles up from the imagination of the *new knitter!*

6. *Show the student how to decrease by knitting two together.*

7. *Show the student how to increase by knitting into the front and the back of a stitch.*

8. *Show the student how to bind off.*

9. *Show the student how to purl.*

My seven-year-old grandson, Jeremy, was learning to knit in the Tried and True way, on a red 10-stitch piece, when he said he wanted to knit a heart for his mom, my daughter, Karen. I was honored to serve as the midwife for this inspiration. Here's how Jeremy knit it. After there were 6

Jeremy's Heart: From
the heart.

rows of garter stitch on the needle, he cut the yarn and I held the stitches for him. Then he cast (knit) on 10 stitches and knit 7 rows. On the next row, we put the held stitches back on the empty needle, and Jeremy knit across them. There were now 20 stitches. Then, he knit 2 together at the beginning and end of the next, and every second row until there were 2 stitches left. He bound off, beamed, and put his heart, which truly had sprung from his soul, in an envelope to give his mom for Valentine's Day. The fact that Jeremy is left-handed didn't present any difficulty.

If you have an opportunity to teach a group of children, here's an exciting idea from Pat Ashforth and Steve Plummer, who call themselves "designers of mathematical knitwear," which has had dazzling results in elementary schools in the United Kingdom. The children knit diagonal garter stitch squares, with a light color as they increase and a dark color as they decrease (or vice versa, since the square can be rotated, which is where the possibilities lie). The teacher makes a template that can be used to determine when to start decreasing. My husband Marvin made a pile of 12-inch square templates folded in quarters to be used as 6-inch square templates for my community-knitting group.

Experience It for Yourself

Two-Tone Gaugeless Diagonal Square

Materials: US 9 needles or size you need to create a cozy fabric. Less than an ounce each of two contrasting colors of worsted weight yarn.

Cast on 3 stitches. You are starting from one corner and you will form two sides of the square as you increase, as follows:

*Knit across, increasing 1 stitch in second stitch (by knitting in the front of the stitch, then in the back before removing from left-hand needle).

Repeat from * every row until each edge measures 6 inches. (You can measure your piece against a 6-inch template.) If you wish to change to a second color, do it here.

Begin decreasing at edges to form the other two sides and opposite corner, as follows:

**Knit 1, knit 2 together, knit across.

Repeat from ** until 3 stitches remain. Knit 2 together, knit 1, pass first stitch over second stitch to end off.

Diagonal Square: A hotbed of design possibilities.

After the squares are knit, more fun and learning begin. There are countless ways to put the squares together to form patterns, depending on the orientation of the light and dark halves of each square. You can see some mind-boggling afghans kids have made and more about the project at www.woollythoughts.com/schools/index.html. Ashforth and Plummer have included an "afghan designer" at their site that lets the potential designers play with light and dark possibilities.

Educator Susan Perrow tells of the power of story in teaching knitting to a group of children: "One of my first successful teaching experiences was using 'story' in a series of knitting lessons. I had only one lesson previous to this with the class in question, and I found them the wildest group of eight year olds I ever had to teach! There were twenty-three children in the class and seventeen were boys. I wanted the children to first make their own knitting needles using dowel rods sharpened at one end with a pencil sharpener and sanded smooth, then a gum nut glued on the other end. However, I was concerned that they would start fighting with the knitting needles, and/or think that knitting was 'uncool' and not be interested in joining the lesson. After much thought (and a sleepless night) I made up a story about two 'magic sticks' that were found by a boy who was always very bored and up to no good. These magic sticks (after a series of incidents in the story) helped this boy make many amazing things, and whenever he had them with him, with the help of a ball of wool, he was never bored again. This story captured the imagination of every member of the class and they couldn't wait to make their own 'magic sticks' and then knit amazing things with them. The knitting lessons for the rest of the term then became the favorite time of the week."[2]

Space between the Loops
Bringing Boys to the Party

I am the mother of four boys. I made a concerted effort to raise my boys to be self-reliant and responsible for their own food and laundry so at least they wouldn't starve or be forced to wear dirty clothes. I wanted them to understand that there is no such thing as women's work or men's work—there's only work. I wanted them to know that nobody likes to do the dishes. (I don't know anybody who does.) I wanted them to have an upbringing that would serve my future daughters-in-law. They were each required to make their own school lunches when they started the second grade; do their own laundry as soon as they could reach the controls on the washer; and take turns on the dishes each night. I taught a couple of them to sew, with my oldest making all of his shorts one summer. (His wife didn't believe him when he said he knew how to work a sewing machine.) They know how to cook their own meals and learned that when a gift is needed in a social situation you can't go wrong with a picture frame. I also taught them all to knit. When each of them approached eight or nine years of age, I would sit down with their small hands and circular needles, the stitches cast on, and begin the lessons. We sang the little verse of "In the house, around the house, through the house and out the house" to learn the movements for making a stitch. I found that using circulars and knitting around made for an easy way to learn as you only have to do the knit stitch and no turning is involved. They happily worked along creating little tube swatches. Number three called his a neck warmer and sported it often that winter. But their knitting careers were short-lived. Perhaps it was just too outside the gender lines for them, or maybe it was too hard for these active kids to sit still for very long, but in any case, none of them "took" to it. But I can say that they do know how to do it. I can say that they have an appreciation for what it is and what it is to me. On occasion they actually bragged to their friends about their mom's work (how often does that happen?), and maybe when they are very old men they will one day say to their grandchildren, "My mother taught me how to knit."

Lead your students to sources. Point to the wisdom of the knitting sages. Bring the students to the well and let them drink. There are excellent books for help and inspiration. (See the Resources section at the end of this book.) Keep a basic library of technique books, stitch libraries, and a couple of pattern collections for inspiration. Have knitting videos on hand. Make them available to your students. Explore your local public library and know what knitting books they have on the shelves. Encourage discovery and creativity. Invite your would-be knitter to go along with you to the yarn shop or a wool festival. Experience texture and color together. Don't forget the Internet and provide a list of your favorite knitting websites. By all means, keep an extra set of needles with a piece of knitting started (as explained in the second "Tried and True Tip") in your knitting bag for the express purpose of impromptu sharing with someone this wonderful work of the hands. Be willing to give it away. Have copies of simple patterns (write one yourself) that you can send on with the learner.

Of course, the reason you're teaching someone to knit is most likely because you're known as a knitter, or they've noticed that you knit and it looks cool. So *do* knit, be cool (in its best sense), and show others the way. Transmit your enthusiasm but be aware that knitting won't be an enthusiasm for everyone. If your students' enthusiasms lie elsewhere, don't take it personally. Let people's enthusiasms lead them to find their god within.

Space between the Loops

Passing It On

Her name is Sarah and when she was twelve years old, she came with her mother to the Needle Worker's Night Out, which was held once a month through the "ladies group" at church. We met in homes, each one bringing her favorite work of the hands, and experienced community together. Sarah came because she liked to be with the ladies but she soon showed an interest in my knitting. I offered to teach her. I kept spare needles and yarn with me, so we moved to a quiet corner and I got her started. She understood quickly. Her grandmother was a knitter and she seemed to carry the knitting gene. We continued the "lessons" during the in-between times at church and delighted in the "I meant to do that" jokes about dropped stitches—"They're not holes; they're buttonholes." Sarah's skills picked up, her interest never waned, and she began to pique the interest of friends at school who also wanted to learn.

We organized a Saturday afternoon knitting "club" and several of her friends attended. Some of the girls were very enthusiastic and some seemed to not really "get it" or never had more than a passing, trendy desire to knit. But that's okay. Learning what's not for you is just as important as learning what is. Patterns were passed out for slippers, a hat, a scarf, a teddy bear sweater, and a baby's layette set. That summer five or six girls learned to knit, but the start of the school year arrived and interests changed. I don't know if any of the other girls still knit, but Sarah does. She went on that next year to participate in a knitting club at her school. She passed on what she knew. The knitting club had as its teacher/sponsor the school's baseball coach. The club members taught him how to knit. What a good sport! Right before me I witnessed the passing on of tradition, skills, and passion. It reminds me of that old hair-color product advertisement—"I told two friends and they told two friends and they told two friends." Today, I enjoy the company of this now fifteen-year-old, who is more of a knitting buddy than a student. I think it is safe to say that she will keep this passion for her life. What an honor to be a part of that.

Another student is my sisterly friend, Michelle. She, too, had a knitting grandmother, and when this grandmother died, Michelle gave me a collection of her knitting needles and other tools. Sometime afterward, Michelle wanted to learn. We met at her house after the children went to school and in a short time she had completed a hat. We laughed about her "way" of knitting. She had a left-handed method of throwing the yarn. It works! I returned her grandmother's needles because Michelle should have them. The privilege of passing it on is mine again. I can't wait till my grandchildren are old enough to work the needles!

The Knitting Community

Knitting groups each have their own personality. I'm a member of an interdenominational group that knits for the community. The core group, about a dozen women, has been meeting for two hours a week for over a year. We've produced, and attracted, many hundreds of items to warm those in need. It's been an important part of my life, not only for the opportunity to spread love and warmth through knitting, but because I'm developing a relationship with a great group of women and relationships with great women in the group.

One day's discussions and revelations included: how solitary knitting used to be; how Sandy made a connection at the ophthalmologist's office with a woman who headed up a homeless shelter—there were kids who needed knitted slippers for walking in the halls and mothers living in these motel rooms with their kids who might like to learn to knit; how to recover yarn from a donated partially knit sweater; learning to play the recorder; shared knitting, family, medical, and travel insights and tips; a field trip with another group to a yarn shop where an employee had knit three *Baby's First Luxuries* sets from my pattern in *Knitter's Stash* by Barbara Albright; planning our first annual "thank-you" lunch; entertaining and entertainment ideas; political debate; and Elaine's delight that an adult grandchild whom she had taught to knit as a child is finding peace in knitting.

I had to leave the group a little early that day for a second try at a root canal. The root turned out to be completely calcified, so I didn't need the work done after all (perhaps a message there about loosening up before it's too late?). At the dentist's office I was involved in knitting encounters over slipper socks. When I walked in with my slipper knitting, an attractive older man smiled at me.

His wife went in to have her root canal done, and he moved across the room to tell me that his grandmother had made him knee-high house socks that laced at the top and fit like a glove. A wonderful memory, he said, how they warmed him. He told stories of the difficulties of life growing up in Italy during World War II when his father, a sailor in the Italian navy, was a prisoner of war.

When I was called in to sit in the dentist's chair, the assistant suggested I keep my knitting in my lap. That's the way to wait for a root canal! When the dentist came in, he saw my knitting and told the story of his wife's wonderful sock pattern that used many colors of yarn. When she wanted to knit the socks for an exchange student living with them, she found she had lost the pattern, which was from an ancient issue of *Good Housekeeping.* Someone at the magazine actually found it and sent her a copy. I said that I'd love to see it. My root canal specialist made a note in his datebook to send it to me, and that he did. That day included "quality" time at the dentist. No root canal, but lots of connection.

I'm finding the development of our community-knitting group, evolving into its own community week by week, an immersion for me in group dynamics that provides insight into my own "story." From what I've read about groups who knit for the community, and my experience in our group, it looks as though its particular venue and the member mix determine the group's unique character. Prayer shawl groups seem to spring from knitters already together in a religious practice. David L. Miller, in an editorial in *The Lutheran,* provided an insight on the phenomenon of knitting prayer shawls, which struck a chord that really resonated with me. He said, "A prayer shawl rests on the back of my office chair, a gift from Bette Shellhorn ... [whose congregation] knits and distributes the shawls to the sick, the struggling, and others in need of special blessing—like me.... Bette says the shawls give the world's many knitters a tangible way to care for others. Fair enough, but there's more here. The tears and longings woven into the sentences of those five hundred-plus notes [asking how to make the prayer shawls and start such a group] express the terrible loneliness of our age—and our craving for connection, for true community.... A prayer shawl hangs on my chair, reminding me that I am not alone."

One pattern,
many choices.

Top Down Shawl:
A comfort project.

A couple of us did knit shawls (I had a recipient in mind for mine), but since we were from diverse backgrounds and affiliations, it became clear (after a group discussion) that it wouldn't work, even if knitting shawls was our sole mission. (See the Resources section for Prayer Shawl resources.)

Experience It for Yourself
Top Down Shawl

This shawl is worked from the center top down in garter stitch. This doesn't have to conform to any particular gauge and any weight yarn can be chosen, as the pattern lends itself to "knit until you run out of yarn, saving enough for the bind-off." Using worsted weight yarn, you will need from 800 to 1,000 yards for an average shawl. Of course the size will vary depending on your needle size.

Cast on 5 stitches.

Knit 2 rows. Mark this side as the Right Side and mark the center stitch.

ALL following rows: Knit 1, yarn over, knit to the center stitch, yarn over, knit center stitch and all remaining stitches.

You must complete a Right Side row and a Wrong Side row to have symmetrical increases.

Work shawl until it is as big as you like, ending with a Wrong Side row and with Right Side facing. Bind off all stitches for a plain edge.

Options for finishing: Keep final stitches on the needle and add fringe by catching 2 stitches with each fringe, work a lace edge or an I-cord edge as you bind off, or add a crocheted border after binding off.

At one point, the dynamic president of a local congregation attended the group for a couple of sessions during which she tried to institute knitting of chemo caps. She had us raffle off one of our afghans to raise money for the Jewish Community Center we used as a base, and she printed raffle tickets that called us a "guild." The chemo cap idea hasn't come together, partly for practical considerations such as yarn availability. Our group members prefer to work from donated yarn—and we use a lot. Plus, no one seemed to want to run with the idea. There are so many needs and so many ideas on how to satisfy them— who to knit for and what to knit. Those of us who care about it were opposed to the label "guild" for our group, since our mission was not to build skills, although we do. We did raffle off the afghan, but we vociferously voted down any idea of raising money through sales of our knits.

The first batch of over 150 mittens, hats, scarves, afghans, and sweaters was split between a local home for battered women and a local outreach service. We received nice thank-you notes from the agencies, but I was somehow unsatisfied at not knowing which kinds of things we knit were best received. I realize that this may be a case of not letting my "children" go. But I think there's more to it. Something in me wants to hear a continuation of the story of our knitting. I want to take cues from it.

We expanded our recipient base this year, adding other agencies, and asked for lists of what they thought was needed. We knit a few group afghans. Our most successful result was put together with a combination of 6- and 12-inch squares. The group started as a result of the 2003 Mitzvah Day, where people came to the Center to do good works. Knitting was one of the activities offered that day. Everyone was asked to knit or crochet a 12-inch square. This presented some problems. Many participants didn't complete their squares. The squares were radically different sizes and shapes! Then our new group spent a lot of time knitting more squares. Putting that afghan together was nothing I'd choose to do again. It took too much compensation to make up for the lack of square coordination. So, for the next Mitzvah Day, Judy, one of our members, came up with the idea of knitting 6-inch squares, for reasons she called "economy of scale." The thinking was that people were more likely to finish them, and there was less room for size variations. I introduced the concept of "gaugeless" squares and provided patterns and templates (of 12-inch newspaper squares, folded into quarters) for squares of both sizes. That did work much better, although we found out that templates don't necessarily ensure consistency in size. And at first I was overwhelmed with the variety of squares and felt sorry that we didn't coordinate colors. But the finished result is a wonderful patchwork of many colors.

Members of our group knit and crocheted more squares and some rectangles, and a couple of us sewed them all together with navy blue yarn in a primitive overcasting stitch. The strange thing is that we couldn't let that one go when we gave our first batch away. We wanted to hold onto it to provide a model for the next Mitzvah Day—and we began knitting more squares to enlarge this true community afghan's warming dimensions.

Experience It for Yourself

Here is a pattern that we use for squares to provide freedom from gauge concerns. (*Note:* Another pattern for the "Two-Tone Gaugeless Diagonal Square" is given earlier in this chapter.) Try these patterns in your own group as you savor the gift of knitting, companionship, and warmth.

Diagonal Square Shaped from the Center: On the needles this square is hidden in plain sight!

Diagonal Square Shaped from the Center

Materials: US 9 needles or size you need to create a cozy fabric. A square takes less than an ounce of worsted weight yarn. If you change colors, the stripe will form as the two sides of a right angle.

Cast on 3 stitches. You are starting from one corner, and all 4 sides of the square are being formed as you increase at the center of every other row—and are held straight across on the needle. When you bind off, the diagonal corner and adjacent edges are released.

Odd Row: Knit across.

Even Row: Knit to center stitch. In center stitch knit in front, then in back, then in front (2 stitches increased in center stitch).

Repeat *Odd* and *Even Rows* until edge measures 6 or 12 inches. Check against paper template. Bind off.

Tip: Place marker before center stitch (which can be a loop of contrasting yarn). On Even Rows, when you get to marker,

197

take it off, knit 1, and replace marker. You are now at the center stitch.

Place a pin on Even Row side so you know you're on an increase row.

Now we have hundreds and hundreds of hand-knits to give out for the impending cold weather. Most members of the group have faith that the knits will wind up warming someone. Each member knit whatever she was moved to during the year, usually taking at least several weeks on a project. New projects that knit up faster are Simple Striped Slippers; and the Warm Ski Band, an adaptation of Mary Walker Phillips's Ski Band from *Step-by-Step Knitting* (knit with two colors held together on a US 11 needle so they can be finished in one meeting). We invite you to visit www.theknittingway.com for updates on our community-knitting story.

The infinite possibilities of two-color combinations on a small number of stitches make both of these projects "knitting candy" that you can knit up quickly as you savor the wonders of color and knitting and the pleasure of warming feet and ears.

Experience It for Yourself

Simple Striped Slippers

Formed from a garter stitch square.

Materials: US 9 needles or size needed to get a gauge of approximately 4 stitches equals 1 inch. Use worsted weight yarn in 2 colors.

Sizes: Child's S *shoe 4–7* (child's M *shoe 8–11,* women's S/M, women's L).

With Color A cast on 24 (28, 36, 40) stitches. Knit two rows. Change to Color B. Knit two rows. Repeat these four rows until piece measures 6 (7, 8, 9) inches. End with last two rows in Color A. Bind off.

With yarn needle threaded with Color A, gather up ridges of right edge of piece and pull tight to form toe, and with right side facing, sew top front seam by sewing cast-on edge to cast-off edge, for approximately 2½ (3½, 4½, 5½) inches from toe. Fasten off.

Fold other end in half (heel) and with a small crochet hook (approximately US F) work single crochet stitches through the edge of both layers from the bottom (folded edge) to the top. Chain 10 for "pull-off-and-on" loop and fasten securely at end of crocheted seam.

If desired, crochet chain and form bow or butterfly as a decoration to fasten at instep.

Simple Striped Slippers: A square from another point of view.

Warm Ski Band

Materials: Two colors of worsted weight yarn, approximately 1 ounce each.

Needles: US 11 or size you need to achieve a cozy fabric.

Gauge: It's more important that you achieve a cozy fabric than try to accurately measure gauge, which is approximately 7 stitches equals 2 inches on the garter stitch section.

Note: If desired, cast on using provisional cast-on method (such as knitting into the purl bumps of a crochet

Warm Ski Band: Worn
in two directions.

chain made with a contrasting yarn with a few chain stitches more than the number of stitches you need to cast on), which will zip right out when you're ready to join the ends together. Then, don't bind off. Kitchener stitch the beginning and ending stitches together.

Using both yarns, held together, cast on 12 stitches.

Work in a knit 2, purl 2 ribbing for 6 inches.

Change to garter stitch (knit every row), increasing in second stitch of next four rows (16 stitches). Knit every row until there are 30 garter stitch ridges (60 rows, approximately 11½ inches).

*Knit 1, knit 2 together (decrease), knit across row. Repeat from * 3 times (12 stitches).

Bind off. Join ends.

Community is a place where we are welcome to just be, to share burdens and joys and to support those who, for a time, might be just a little weaker. It's a place to share, gain wisdom, learn, and teach, and it provides immeasurable opportunity for the making of mentors. Come to your community with the sense of giving.

These communities are springing up everywhere. There are neighborhood groups; office, church, school, and college groups; knitting communities based in the yarn shops; and communities based in pubs. There are commuter groups (those who daily travel in trains together). Find one near you or start your own. Possible venues are community rooms where you live, church or synagogue or mosque facilities, and local libraries (which often encourage such groups). Or, gather some friends in your home, a coffeehouse, or a bar. Knit in public and make new friends. It's easy these days to connect with other knitters and others who are anxious to learn. It seems to be the Spirit of the Times. The spirit is seen on the streets of cities around the country at the Knit Outs & Crochet, an event that was started by the Craft Yarn Council of America in the late '90s in New York City and has mushroomed each fall since.

You can see the spirit in the communities coming together through the Internet, where members meet every day and arrange times and locations to meet face to face. In addition to the big online communities, there are special-interest groups such as Knitting Novices, Ample-Knitters, Knitted Lace, and the Sock Lists, and they stretch across age and gender barriers. The guys are getting in on the community action, too, forming their own support groups. There are even groups based around a common project, known as "Knit Alongs." Take your pick and join in.

The continuation of this community, this connection, and this Knitting Way is the path to the continuation of knitting itself. We each carry a responsibility to pass it on, to see that it remains a craft of heart and soul to those who come after us. Connecting our knitting stories to communities and individuals makes them a part of our story, and us a part of theirs. It is the way that heart to heart and hand to hand the knitting will survive and continue to be a place of warmth, safety, spirit, and nurturing of the soul.

Space between the Loops
The State of Knit
What is this place where mind meets hand and hand meets wool? Where loop upon loop brings form and beauty. Where function grows from a single strand. It is the state of Knit.

Knitting is a miracle. One strand of wool grows and blossoms into a fabric of warmth and beauty. Like the single vine of peas in the garden that starts as one tiny leaf and expands into a great long vine carrying graceful tendrils and burgeoning pods of fruit. So grows the knitting. First one row, then another, next a twist and a corner turned: A sweater blooms. A mitten patch breaks the sod. The socks wave in the breeze.

There is warmth in knitting, both physical (from a comfy finished sweater) and spiritual (that feeling of satisfaction of a work in progress). Knitting gives a connection to the land, to the past. Rolling hills, green meadows, and pastures filled with sheep all rumble around in the brain as each stitch passes. Grandma, Great Auntie: They knitted, too, for family, for soldiers, for themselves, for joy. History repeats.

Comfort is reaped from the act. Time spent at a sickbed made more bearable by the gentle motion. The click of needles, the touch of the wool—both soothe the soul. Time is marked. This hat was made on that vacation to the Grand Canyon. Do you remember those colors? Mother finished this shawl just before she passed away. What a treasure!

Birthdays, weddings, babies all marked by the knitting. Stitch upon stitch, loop upon loop, row upon row. Miracle, warmth, joy, land, past, comfort, time, Knit!

Conclusion

Continuing the Story

Tea, Recipes, and Haiku for the Journey

We've come to the last row, and it's time to bind off. Our book is finished, but our stories never will be. For the past two years, Linda and I have met every Monday night to wind ourselves around each other's story. We have learned things about each other that we may have otherwise never known. Patternworks is the reason we even know each other, for, though we are knitters, without that Yarn Paradise our paths probably never would have crossed, and we wouldn't have been asked to explore the Knitting Way. We have created a story, now, that we both share, one filled with laughter and tears, husbands, families, politics, church, synagogue, and, of course, the knitting.

We invite you to continue on with us in this knitting story that surrounds all those who wield the wood and wool, those who share spirit. Cast on new stitches with us as we intend to continue to meet, this time just to be knitters together instead of writers, a new turn along the way. Join us. Have tea with us. We have enjoyed many of the fine teas from Harney and Sons and Ten Ren's Tea House, brought back from our lovely knitting train trip to Chinatown with Sharyn and Karen. We'd like to share these recipes with you, a taste of the many goodies that passed over our lips (and straight to the hips), partly in the hopes that we may become a small part of your story. We'd love to hear from you at www.theknittingway.com.

Carrot Pecan Cake

From Anna Quandt, Janice's mother

1¼ cups vegetable oil
1 tsp salt
2 cups granulated sugar
2 cups all purpose flour
2 tsp baking powder
3 cups grated raw carrots
1 tsp baking soda
1 cup chopped pecans
2 tsp cinnamon
4 eggs

Combine oil and sugar and mix well. Sift dry ingredients together.

Sift ½ dry ingredients into the oil and sugar mix. Add the remaining dry ingredients to the batter alternately with the eggs. Fold in the carrots and nuts. Pour into a lightly oiled 10-inch tube (or Bundt) pan. Bake at 325 degrees for 1 hour and 10 minutes. Cool in the pan for 10 minutes before removing to a plate.

Glaze

Mix ¾ cup of confectioner sugar with approximately 5 Tbsp of orange juice and ½ tsp vanilla. Add the orange juice 1 Tbsp at a time until the glaze is at a thick but pourable consistency. Add more or less, as you desire. Drizzle over warm cake.

Bubby (Grandma) Cookies

A recipe "from the ages," courtesy of Sylvia Lerner (a member of the Audrey Morgenstern Knitting and Crocheting Group, the community knitting group to which Linda belongs)

½ lb butter or margarine
1 tsp vanilla
1 tsp baking powder
1 cup brown sugar
1 egg
3½ cups flour
2 Tbsp sour cream

In a mixing bowl, combine all the above ingredients and work until a smooth, elastic ball of dough is formed.

Topping

2 Tbsp cinnamon
2–3 Tbsp sugar
1 cup chopped walnuts
1 beaten egg *in another dish*

Pinch off small chunks of dough; roll into balls; flatten and dip each one into beaten egg and then into chopped nuts mixed with sugar and cinnamon. Place on greased cookie sheet, leaving a little space between each cookie. Bake at 350 degrees for 20 minutes or until golden brown. Remove from pan while hot and place on a rack to cool.

A Morsel of Knitting Life

One of the last "experiments" we attempted was a foray into the writing of haiku and renku. Japanese haiku, that short verse that touches deeply, provides us with snapshots of nature in which the observer (you or I) is portrayed as a participant in nature, not the central figure—a spiritual outlook. Generally it is a 3-line poem, the first line containing 5 syllables, the second line containing 7, and the third line containing 5. However, this is not a rigid

205

rule and arrangements of 3-4-3, and others are also an option. Renku is the linking of many haiku verses and was originally a party game where puns and humor collide. These are verses that provide a morsel rather than a slice of life. We discovered several Internet sites that linked knitting and haiku. Linda and I tried our hand at it. We independently wrote three haikus, no prearranged ideas, except that it was to reflect knitting. We then linked them into a renku and were pleasantly surprised at our result.

Straight line turns to loop
Lined up distant hills beckon
The heart through the hands.

Stick of wood holds now
And the tree from which it came
Time is found therein.

Basket of color
Bathed in winter warmth and light
Gives a gift of soul.

A stitch passes
Ripened fabric heavy
Yarn exhausting.

Wind at window
Loop breaks free to flow
A river runs.

Kinky reclaimed skein
From an unloved sweater
Bathed it relaxes.

It is our hope that you will find, claim, and reclaim the story that you hold within. Keep faith, carry the Light, think of all knitters everywhere when you have your knitting in hand, and always be open to the deep and wondrous places of your soul.

Appendix

Letter Patterns for da Vinci Message Seaman's Scarf

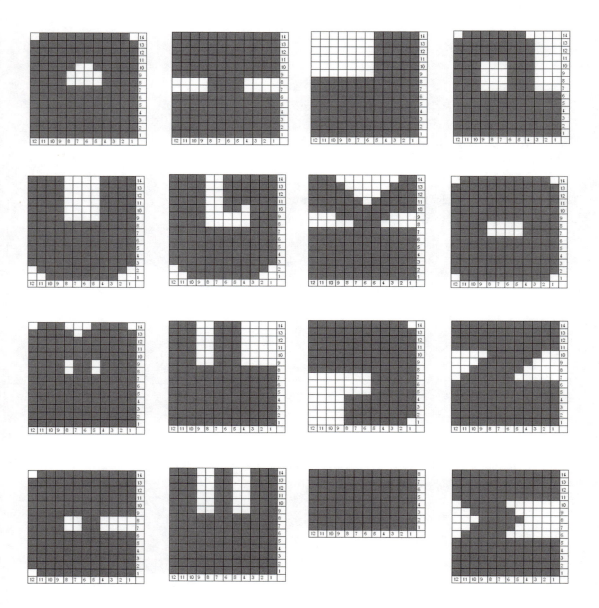

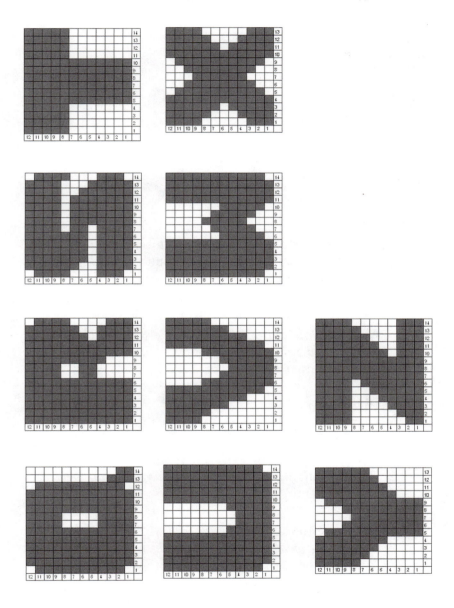

Notes

Introduction

1. Barbara Albright, ed., *Knitter's Stash: Favorite Patterns from America's Yarn Shops* (Loveland, Colo.: Interweave Press, 2001), p. 112.

2. Debbie Stoller, *Stitch 'n' Bitch: The Knitter's Handbook* (New York: Workman Publishing, 2003), p. 39.

3. Marion Woodman, *Addiction to Perfection: The Still Unravished Bride—A Psychological Study* (Toronto, Canada: Inner City Books, 1982), p. 26.

Chapter 1

1. Cris Carusi, "Knitting," posted at the Nebraska Sustainable Agriculture Society (NSAS) website, www.nebsusag.org/newsletters/poetry61.htm.

2. Brenda Euland, *Strength to Your Sword Arm: Selected Writings* (Duluth, Minn.: Holy Cow! Press, 1993), p. 210.

3. Thomas Moore, *Care of the Soul: A Guide for Cultivating Depth and Sacredness in Everyday Life* (New York: HarperCollins, 1992), p. 5.

4. Alison Ellen, *Hand Knitting: New Directions* (Wiltshire, U.K.: Crowood Press, 2002), p. 27.

5. Betty Smith, *A Tree Grows in Brooklyn* (New York: HarperCollins, 2001), p. 419.

6. Helene Rush, "Quick-to-Knit Vest" in *More Maine Sweaters: 30 Original Designs in Wool, Cotton, Silk,*

and Alpaca (Camden, Maine: Down East Books, 1987), p. 83.

Chapter 2

1. Janna Levin, *How the Universe Got Its Spots: Diary of a Finite Time in a Finite Space* (New York: Anchor Books, 2002), p. 65.
2. René Dubos, *A God Within* (New York: Scribner, 1972), p. 215.
3. Steven Harrison, *Doing Nothing: Coming to the End of the Spiritual Search* (New York: J. P. Tarcher/Putnam, 1997), p. 91.
4. Woodman, *Addiction to Perfection,* p. 8.
5. Reprinted from Lynn G. Underwood, PhD, Fetzer Institute, and Jeannne A. Teresi, EdD, PhD, Hebrew Home for the Aged at Riverdale and Columbia University Stroud Center, "The Daily Spiritual Experience Scale: Development, Theoretical Description, Reliability, Exploratory Factor Analysis, and Preliminary Construct Validity Using Health-Related Data" (paper), with permission of Lynn G. Underwood, PhD.

Chapter 3

1. This piece can be found on artist Julio Mateo's website, www.mateo.net.
2. Mary Thomas, *Mary Thomas's Book of Knitting Patterns* (New York: Dover Publications, 1972), p. 1.
3. Marion Milner, *A Life of One's Own* (Los Angeles: J. P. Tarcher, 1981), p. 15.
4. Thomas, *Mary Thomas's Book of Knitting Patterns,* p. 5.
5. Janez Strehovec, "Text as Loop: On Visual and Kinetic Textuality" in *Afterimage,* July–August 2003. Available online at www.findarticles.com/p/articles/mi_m2479/is_1_31.
6. Julia Cameron, *The Artist's Way: A Spiritual Path to*

Higher Creativity (New York: J. P. Tarcher/Putnam, 2002), p. 107.

Chapter 4

1. Richard Rutt, *A History of Hand Knitting* (Loveland, Colo.: Interweave Press, 1987), p. 161.
2. Deirdre McQuillan, *The Aran Sweater* (Belfast, U.K.: Appletree Press, 1993), p. 16.
3. Rutt, *A History of Hand Knitting,* p. 199.
4. Vibeke Lind, *Knitting in the Nordic Tradition* (Asheville, N.C.: Lark Books, 1991), p. 7.
5. Priscilla A. Gibson-Roberts, *Knitting in the Old Way: Designs and Techniques from Ethnic Sweaters* (Fort Collins, Colo.: Nomad Press, 2004), p. 4.
6. June Hemmons Hiatt, *Principles of Knitting: Methods and Techniques of Hand Knitting* (New York: Simon and Schuster, 1988), p. 117.
7. Elizabeth Zimmermann, *Knitting without Tears: Basic Techniques and Easy-to-Follow Directions for Garments to Fit All Sizes* (New York: Scribner, 1971), p. 52.
8. Elizabeth Zimmermann, *Knitter's Almanac: Projects for Each Month of the Year* (New York: Dover Publications, 1981), p. 1.
9. Robert Aitken, *Zen Wave: Bashō's Haiku and Zen.* Foreword by W. S. Merwin (Washington, D.C.: Shoemaker & Hoard, 2003), p. 13.
10. Melanie D. Falick, *Knitting in America* (New York: Artisan, 1996), p. 60.
11. David Rucker, "Event at the River," in *Tales in Time,* vol. 2 (Franklin, Ind.: Bookman Publishing, 2004), pp. 92–93.

Chapter 5

1. John Briggs and F. David Peat, *Seven Life Lessons of Chaos: Timeless Wisdom from the Science of Change* (New York: HarperCollins, 1999), p. 65.

2. Emi Nakamura, interviewed in the Fushiginoiroito project. Visit www.knitjapan.co.uk.

3. Sue Bender, *Everyday Sacred: A Woman's Journey Home* (San Francisco: HarperSanFrancisco, 1976), pp. 141–44.

Chapter 6

1. Pauline Burton, from the "In Transit" section of *OutLoud: An Anthology of Poetry from OutLoud Readings* (Hong Kong: XtraLoud Press, 2002), p. 30. Burton's poem can be found online at www.asian voices.org/voices/freight.htm.

2. Jacob Needleman, *Time and the Soul: Where Has All the Meaningful Time Gone—and Can We Get It Back?* (San Francisco: Berrett-Koehler , 2003), p. 38.

3. Maurice Nicoll, *Living Time and the Integration of the Life* (Boulder: Shambhala, 1976), p. 126.

4. Ibid., p. 227.

5. Pam England, "Holding the Space, A Doula's Best Gift," available online at www.birthingfromwithin .com/holdingthespace.html.

6. Tilden Edwards, *Living Simply through the Day: Spiritual Survival in a Complex Age* (New York: Paulist Press, 1977), p. 74.

Chapter 7

1. Bernard Graves, Hiram Trust, 1996, in an interview found online at www.hiramtrust.org.uk/Publications Tables.htm.

2. Neil Douglas-Klotz, "The Natural Breath: Towards Further Dialogue between Western Somatic and Eastern Spiritual Approaches to the Body Awareness of Breathing," *The Healing Breath* 2, no. 2 (2000), p. 10.

3. The Arthritis Victoria Organization for Musculo-Skeletal Health, www.nevdgp.org.au/geninf/ ArthritisF/management/exercise/pause.htm, offers other good tips for keeping your body in tune.

Chapter 8

1. Moore, *Care of the Soul,* p. 11.
2. Ernest Kurtz and Ketcham Katherine, *The Spirituality of Imperfection: Storytelling and the Search for Meaning* (New York: Bantam Books, 2002), p. 102.
3. C. S. Lewis, "Religion: Reality or Substitute?" in *Christian Reflections* (Grand Rapids, Mich.: W. B. Eerdman's, 1995), p. 37.
4. Kay Lindahl, *The Sacred Art of Listening: Forty Reflections for Cultivating a Spiritual Practice* (Woodstock, Vt.: SkyLight Paths, 2002), pp. 3, 82.
5. Judy Allen's article can be found online at www.pyramus.com/acim/topics/forgive/unravel.htm.

Chapter 9

1. Quoted in Phil Cousineau, *Once and Future Myths: The Power of Ancient Stories in Modern Times* (Berkeley: Conari Press, 2001), p. 117.
2. Susan Perrow, "The Power of Story," found on the Swaraj Foundation website, www.swaraj.org.

Resources

Each of these books and videos contributes something to our knitting depth and is consulted again and again. It's a delight and an education to look at the world of knitting through these authors' delving, caring eyes and minds, and discover how to do things in new ways—and have them available to us in the comfort of our knitting chairs. Sometimes a different emphasis and focus or a different illustration will suddenly make one of our bugaboos clear. This is far from a complete list, but we hope it will be a suggested guide to creating and/or adding to your library of knitting wisdom.

General Knitting

Allen, Pam. *Knitting for Dummies.* New York: Hungry Minds, 2002.
A basic "how to" that is clear and informative.

Budd, Ann. *The Knitter's Handy Book of Patterns: Basic Designs in Multiple Sizes & Gauges.* Loveland, Colo.: Interweave Press, 2002.
Basic templates for mittens, gloves, hats, tams, scarves, socks, vests, and sweaters, sized for infants to large adults in yarn weights from baby to bulky.

Burnette, Cheryl. *Sweater 101*: How to Plan Sweaters That Fit ... and Organize Your Knitting Life at the Same Time.* Center Harbor, N.H.: Patternworks, 1991.
This "workshop in a folder" is an invaluable aid for

creating successful sweaters that fit. Cheryl is the queen of making it all clear and keeping it simple.

Buss, Katharina. *Big Book of Knitting.* New York: Sterling Publishing Company, 1999.
A beautiful presentation of techniques from the basic to the esoteric.

Falick, Melanie. *Kids Knitting: Projects for Kids of All Ages.* New York: Artisan, 1998.
Shows what can be accomplished when beginners are guided by a first-rate designer. Irresistible projects for kids from six to ninety-nine. Every process from winding a ball of wool to finishing is presented with Kristin Nicholas's clear and cozy illustrations.

Fee, Jacqueline. *The Sweater Workshop: Knit Creative Seam-Free Sweaters on Your Own with Any Yarn.* Camden, Maine: Down East Books, 2002.
Full of knitting wisdom, ideas and techniques for knitting seamless sweaters from the bottom up.

Melville, Sally. *The Knitting Experience: Inspiration and Instruction—The Knit Stitch.* Sioux Falls, S.D.: XRX Books, 2002.
Melville starts the knitter at the beginning, and her expertise is abundantly shared in these two volumes. Future works are in the making.

———. *The Knitting Experience: Becoming Intuitive—The Purl Stitch.* Sioux Falls, S.D.: XRX Books, 2003.

Modesitt, Annie. *Confessions of a Knitting Heretic.* South Orange, N.J.: Modeknit Press, 2004.
Unconventional knitting advice from a self-confident knitter that may help you see your knitting in a new way.

Newton, Deborah. *Designing Knitwear.* Newtown, Conn.: Taunton Press, 1998.
A generous book in which a respected knitwear designer gives her techniques, tips, and secrets, which Newton says are "intended to give you a design system to borrow partly or entirely until developing your own."

Righetti, Maggie. *Knitting in Plain English.* New York: St. Martin's Press, 1986.
Sage and witty advice from a veteran yarn shop owner.

Stanley, Montse. *Knitter's Handbook: A Comprehensive Guide to the Principles and Techniques of Handknitting.* Pleasantville, N.Y.: Reader's Digest, 1999.
A comprehensive guide from the author's distinctive viewpoint.

Stoller, Debbie. *Stitch 'N' Bitch: The Knitter's Handbook.* New York: Workman Publishing, 2003.
This is a "cool," clear, how-to-knit book that appeals to young knitters.

Thomas, Mary. *Mary Thomas's Knitting Book.* New York: Dover Publications, 1972.
So much is packed into this little book that it might be the one you take to the desert island (with its companion, *Mary Thomas's Book of Knitting Patterns*).

Threads Magazine. *Colorful Knitwear Design.* Newtown, Conn.: Taunton Press, 1994.
A treasury of ideas and techniques for knitting in multi-color.

Vogue Knitting: The Ultimate Knitting Book. New York: Sixth & Spring Books, 2002.
A valuable encyclopedia of information.

Wiseman, Nancie M. *The Knitter's Book of Finishing Techniques.* Woodenville, Wash.: Martingale Press, 2002.
Well presented and easy to understand with good photos and clear drawings.

Zilboorg, Anna. *Knitting for Anarchists.* Petaluma, Calif.: Unicorn Books, 2002.
A refreshing and informative manifesto on taking control of your knitting.

Zimmermann, Elizabeth. *Knitting Without Tears: Basic Techniques and Easy-to-Follow Directions for Garments to Fit All Sizes.* New York: Scribner, 1971.
The book that stopped the tears of countless knitters.

———. *Elizabeth Zimmermann's Knitter's Almanac: Projects for Each Month of the Year.* New York: Dover Publications, 1981.
A project for each month of the year. A knitter shouldn't have to go through the year without it.

———. *Elizabeth Zimmermann's Knitting Workshop.* Pittsville, Wisc.: Schoolhouse Press, 1981.
A course in knitting from the beginning that includes Zimmermann wisdom and patterns for the Surprise Jacket, the Nalgar (raglan spelled backwards), the Heart Hat, the Pi Shawl, and more.

———. *Knitting Around, or, Knitting without a License.* Pittsville, Wisc.: Schoolhouse Press, 1989.
Elizabeth's personal reminiscences are as captivating as her knitting philosophy and constructions.

Stitch Treasuries

We believe that you can't have too many of these. Stitch patterns are the daily bread of knitting.

Stanfield, Lesley. *The New Knitting Stitch Library.* Asheville, N.C.: Lark Books, 1998.
I love the thumbnail photo for each stitch, organized by type, which makes it easy to find just the one you need.

Thomas, Mary. *Mary Thomas's Book of Knitting Patterns.* New York: Dover Publications, 1972.
The completion of Mary Thomas's legacy to knitters.

Walker, Barbara G. *A Treasury of Knitting Patterns.* Pittsville, Wisc.: Schoolhouse Press, 1998.
The first of Walker's classic treasuries that are, themselves, treasures. Walker accompanies the stitches with comments and suggestions for using them to best advantage.

———. *A Second Treasury of Knitting Patterns.* Pittsville, Wisc.: Schoolhouse Press, 1998.

———. *Charted Knitting Designs: A Third Treasury of Knitting Patterns.* Pittsville, Wisc.: Schoolhouse Press, 1998.

———. *A Fourth Treasury of Knitting Patterns: Sampler Knitting Augmented.* Pittsville, Wisc.: Schoolhouse Press, 2001.

Traditional (Folk) Knitting

Some of these books contain extensive stitch treasuries, as noted with an asterisk.

Bush, Nancy. *Folk Socks: The History and Techniques of Handknitted Footwear.* Loveland, Colo.: Interweave Press, 1995.
Patterns for the traditional socks of the world, including delectable tidbits of history and culture.

———. *Folk Knitting in Estonia: A Garland of Symbolism, Tradition, and Technique.* Loveland, Colo.: Interweave Press, 2000.
The fruit of four years of research.

Feitelson, Ann. *The Art of Fair Isle Knitting: History, Technique, Color, and Pattern.* Loveland, Colo.: Interweave Press, 1997.
The scoop on the history and techniques of Fair Isle knitting from a passionate and precise historian and knitter.

Gibson-Roberts, Priscilla A. *Ethnic Socks and Stockings: A Compendium of Eastern Technique and Design.* Sioux Falls, S.D.: XRX Books, 1997.
A feast of socks, including an East/West hybrid developed by Gibson-Roberts that combines the best of both worlds for a perfect-fitting sock that's knit from the toe up.

———. *Knitting in the Old Way: Designs and Techniques from Ethnic Sweaters.* Fort Collins, Colo.: Nomad Press, 2004.
A loving presentation of the ways of our knitting forebears.

Harmony Guide. *220 Aran Stitches and Patterns—Volume 5.* Pomfret, Vt.: Trafalgar Square Publishing, 1998.*
A basic must-have.

Khmeleva, Galina, and Carol R. Noble. *Gossamer Webs: The History and Techniques of Orenburg Lace Shawls.*

Loveland, Colo.: Interweave Press, 1998.
A wonderful account of the history of Orenburg's famous knitted lace shawls, with charts and tips for designing and knitting one yourself.

Lewandowski, Marcia. *Folk Mittens: Techniques and Patterns for Handknitted Mittens.* Loveland, Colo.: Interweave Press, 1997.
Patterns for forty-eight mitten styles.

Lind, Vibeke. *Knitting in the Nordic Tradition.* Asheville, N.C.: Lark Books, 1991.
All sorts of useful techniques used in traditional Nordic knitting are clearly shown.

McGregor, Sheila. *Traditional Fair Isle Knitting.* New York: Dover Publications, 2003.*
We're glad that McGregor's Fair Isle and Scandinavian treasuries are back in print.

———. *Traditional Scandinavian Knitting.* New York: Dover Publications, 2004.*

Oberle, Cheryl. *Folk Shawls: 25 Knitting Patterns and Tales from Around the World.* Loveland, Colo.: Interweave Press, 2000.
The Faroe Islands, Ireland, Japan, the American Heartland, Iceland, Victorian England, Russia, Scotland, Mexico, South America, Norway, Native America, the Himalayas, and Spain are all included in this wonderful collection of patterns and traditions.

Thompson, Gladys. *Patterns for Guernseys, Jerseys, and Arans: Fishermen's Sweaters from the British Isles.* New York: Dover Publications, 2003.*
One of Elizabeth Zimmermann's beloved references.

Upitis, Lizbeth. *Latvian Mittens: Traditional Designs and Techniques.* Pittsville, Wisc.: Schoolhouse Press, 1997.
Challenging and wonderful and worth making at least one pair.

Waterman, Martha. *Traditional Knitted Lace Shawls.* Loveland, Colo.: Interweave Press, 1998.*
A course in designing, caring for, and wearing shawls of all types and shapes for knitters of every level.

Prayer Shawls

Jorgensen, Susan S., and Susan S. Izard. *Knitting into the Mystery: A Guide to the Shawl-Knitting Ministry.* Harrisburg, Pa.: Morehouse Publishing, 2003.

Thinking Outside the Box

And for the very curious and willing ...

New, Debbie. *Unexpected Knitting.* Pittsville, Wisc.: Schoolhouse Press, 2003.
We were blown away by this mind expander! An exhilarating look into knitting that will take you to new places. Original concepts and techniques for creating knitted works of art, with instructions for adventurous knitters.

Videos

Knitting Workshop with Elizabeth Zimmermann. Pittsville, Wisc.: Schoolhouse Press, 1987.
Set of two videocassettes. The visual companion to her book (see above, under General Knitting).

Elizabeth Zimmermann's Knitting Glossary with Elizabeth Zimmermann & Meg Swansen. Pittsville, Wisc.: Schoolhouse Press, 1987.
Set of two videocassettes. EZ's techniques in one convenient source.

Knitting Around with Elizabeth Zimmermann and Meg Swansen. Pittsville, Wisc.: Schoolhouse Press, 1992.
Set of three videocassettes. Let these two women come into your knitting space and experience their warm and loving connection to each other and to you. Companion work to the book of the same name (see above, under General Knitting).

Brunette, Cheryl. *Finishing 101: Easy Finishing for Pullover Sweaters.* Marrowstone Knitting School, 1992.
One videocassette. Available directly from Cheryl: P.O. Box 112, Nordland, WA 98358. Cheryl shows you how to put a sweater together like a professional, and how to plan for finishing success from the moment you cast on.

Websites

Knitting Help

www.ample-knitters.com
  An online community for knitters of "all sizes of large."

www.dnt-inc.com/barhtmls/knittech.html
  Animated demonstrations of basic techniques.

www.helpinghandsprogram.org
  Information on becoming a knitting mentor in a school.

www.kaleidesigns.com/crochet/knitting
  Links to good, free patterns and information for knitting for the community.

www.kidscanmakeit.com/AC0023.htm
  Finger knitting instructions using five fingers.

www.knitting.about.com
  Knitting resources and patterns.

www.knittinghelp.com
  Online video clips that show a large variety of techniques.

www.socknitters.com
  A sock-knitting resource including patterns and techniques.

www.tata-tatao.to/knit/e-home.html
  Illustrations and instructions for knitting basics and deciphering Japanese symbols and charts.

www.woolworks.org
  Knitting information, patterns, and links.

Magazines

www.interweaveknits.com
  Includes knitting resources and free patterns.

www.knittersreview.com
  An informative online knitting magazine.

www.knittinguniverse.com
  Includes how-to video clips for basics and a yarn shop finder.

www.knitty.com
  Cool online knitting magazine with free original patterns.

www.tkga.com
   Homepage of The Knitting Guild Association, which publishes Cast On magazine. Includes local guild connections and links to other resources.

www.vogueknitting.com
   Includes illustrated learn-to-knit basics in the "Tech" section.

Acknowledgments

I'm grateful to Maura Shaw and Janice MacDaniels who made this book possible and a reality. Maura believed in me to carry through her idea for a book using knitting as a spiritual tool, then encouraged, professionally edited with care, and gently prodded so that *The Knitting Way* could come to be. It has been an honor and a pleasure to work with Janice, who unfailingly expresses her deep faith in soul-finding ways, and helped me understand what spirituality is all about. I had the luxury of being able to trust in the talents and intentions of Janice and Maura. They never let *The Knitting Way* down. Then Sarah McBride shepherded the book to its final form with intelligence and sensitivity.

To my husband and partner, Marvin Skolnik, who worked with me through thick and thin to make Patternworks what it was—and is still by my side. Marvin, thanks for taking and lovingly processing the photographs for this book and for keeping me going with your gourmet meals. How can I ever thank you?

To my Grandma Anesblott, who taught me to knit.

To my mother and father, without whom I wouldn't be here today. To my children and grandchildren who continue to show me the meaning of life.

To everyone who worked at Patternworks and provided the lifeblood that brought the Yarn Paradise to life. Without your work, there would have not been a Yarn Paradise and I would not have had the chance to write this book. Thank you, Amy Steidl-Olson for relocating with Patternworks to New Hampshire and carrying the flame.

To Richard Deon, the graphic artist whose talent and generous spirit allowed me to fully participate in the creation of the Patternworks catalog. It was my first close encounter with talent of that magnitude, and an initiation into the miracle of teamwork, as each catalog came together. Richard advised me to approach the writing of this book as I would knit a sweater: Knit up all the string and then neaten up the ends. That's just about right.

To everyone whose life has touched mine, and whom I wrote about in *The Knitting Way*. Thank you to the members of the Audrey Morgenstern Knitting Group for being part of my life each week and for knitting projects in this book. To Gway-Yuang (Karen) Ko and Sharyn Faranda for making the journey from trusted employees to valued knitting friends.

—Linda Skolnik

To Maura Shaw for without her there would be no book. Thank you for your patience and gentle hand of guidance in getting this done.

To my husband, Gene, for his encouragement and understanding. Thank you for all of your help in giving me time to work. Love you.

To my children and grandchildren for reminding me that there are things that matter in a hundred years. Thank you for being you and your acceptance of my knitting and serving as inspirations.

To my parents for raising me in a home of faith and creativity. Thank you, Mom and Dad.

To Marvin Skolnik for his talented eye and photographic skills. Thank you for sharing Linda with me and pulling many nights of kitchen duty.

To Karen Ko and Sharyn Faranda for all of their cheerleading and support. Thank you for being my knitting buddies.

225

Acknowledgments

To the members of the Audrey Morgenstern Knitting Group for their input and suggestions. Thank you for your part in this book.

To Linda for being my friend and sharing her life with me. Thank you.

—Janice MacDaniels

AVAILABLE FROM BETTER BOOKSTORES.
TRY YOUR BOOKSTORE FIRST.

Children's Spiritual Biography

MULTICULTURAL, NONDENOMINATIONAL, NONSECTARIAN

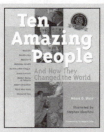

Ten Amazing People
And How They Changed the World
by Maura D. Shaw; Foreword by Dr. Robert Coles
Full-color illus. by Stephen Marchesi

For ages 7 & up

Black Elk • Dorothy Day • Malcolm X • Mahatma Gandhi • Martin Luther King, Jr. • Mother Teresa • Janusz Korczak • Desmond Tutu • Thich Nhat Hanh • Albert Schweitzer

This vivid, inspirational, and authoritative book will open new possibilities for children by telling the stories of how ten of the past century's greatest leaders changed the world in important ways.

8½ x 11, 48 pp, HC, Full-color illus., ISBN 1-893361-47-0 **$17.95** *For ages 7 & up*

Spiritual Biographies for Young People—For ages 7 and up

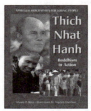
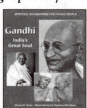
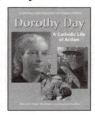
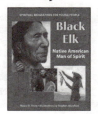

Black Elk: Native American Man of Spirit
by Maura D. Shaw; Full-color illus. by Stephen Marchesi
Through historically accurate illustrations and photos, inspiring age-appropriate activities, and Black Elk's own words, this colorful biography introduces children to a remarkable person who ensured that the traditions and beliefs of his people would not be forgotten.
6¾ x 8¾, 32 pp, HC, Full-color illus., ISBN 1-59473-043-1 **$12.99**

Dorothy Day: A Catholic Life of Action
by Maura D. Shaw; Full-color illus. by Stephen Marchesi
Introduces children to one of the most inspiring women of the twentieth century, a down-to-earth spiritual leader who saw the presence of God in every person she met. Includes practical activities, a timeline, and a list of important words to know.
6¾ x 8¾, 32 pp, HC, Full-color illus., ISBN 1-59473-011-3 **$12.99**

Gandhi: India's Great Soul
by Maura D. Shaw; Full-color illus. by Stephen Marchesi
There are a number of biographies of Gandhi written for young readers, but this is the only one that balances a simple text with illustrations, photographs, and activities that encourage children and adults to talk about how to make changes happen without violence. Introduces children to important concepts of freedom, equality, and justice among people of all backgrounds and religions.
6¾ x 8¾, 32 pp, HC, Full-color illus., ISBN 1-893361-91-8 **$12.95**

Thich Nhat Hanh: Buddhism in Action
by Maura D. Shaw; Full-color illus. by Stephen Marchesi
Warm illustrations, photos, age-appropriate activities, and Thich Nhat Hanh's own poems introduce a great man to children in a way they can understand and enjoy. Includes a list of important Buddhist words to know.
6¾ x 8¾, 32 pp, HC, Full-color illus., ISBN 1-893361-87-X **$12.95**

Spirituality

Autumn: A Spiritual Biography of the Season
Edited by Gary Schmidt and Susan M. Felch; Illustrations by Mary Azarian
Autumn is a season of fruition and harvest, of thanksgiving and celebration of abundance and goodness of the earth. But it is also a season that starkly and realistically encourages us to see the limitations of our time. Warm and poignant pieces by Wendell Berry, David James Duncan, Robert Frost, A. Bartlett Giamatti, Kimiko Hahn, P. D. James, Julian of Norwich, Garret Keizer, Tracy Kidder, Anne Lamott, May Sarton, and many others rejoice in autumn as a time of preparation and reflection. 6 x 9, 320 pp, 5 b/w illus., HC, ISBN 1-59473-005-9 **$22.99**

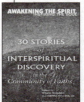

Awakening the Spirit, Inspiring the Soul
30 Stories of Interspiritual Discovery in the Community of Faiths
Edited by Brother Wayne Teasdale and Martha Howard, MD; Foreword by Joan Borysenko, PhD
Thirty original spiritual mini-biographies that showcase the varied ways that people come to faith—and what that means—in today's multi-religious world.
6 x 9, 224 pp, HC, ISBN 1-59473-039-3 **$21.99**

Winter: A Spiritual Biography of the Season
Edited by Gary Schmidt and Susan M. Felch; Illustrations by Barry Moser
Delves into the varied feelings that winter conjures in us, calling up both the barrenness and the beauty of the natural world in wintertime. Includes selections by Will Campbell, Rachel Carson, Annie Dillard, Donald Hall, Ron Hansen, Jane Kenyon, Jamaica Kincaid, Barry Lopez, Kathleen Norris, John Updike, E. B. White, and many others. "This outstanding anthology features top-flight nature and spirituality writers on the fierce, inexorable season of winter.... Remarkably lively and warm, despite the icy subject." —*Publishers Weekly* Starred Review
6 x 9, 288 pp, 6 b/w illus., Deluxe PB w/flaps, ISBN 1-893361-92-6 **$18.95**; HC, ISBN 1-893361-53-5 **$21.95**

The Alphabet of Paradise: An A–Z of Spirituality for Everyday Life
by Howard Cooper 5 x 7¾, 224 pp, Quality PB, ISBN 1-893361-80-2 **$16.95**

Creating a Spiritual Retirement: A Guide to the Unseen Possibilities in Our Lives
by Molly Srode 6 x 9, 208 pp, b/w photos, Quality PB, ISBN 1-59473-050-42 **$14.99**;
HC, ISBN 1-893361-75-6 **$19.95**

The Geography of Faith: Underground Conversations on Religious, Political and Social Change *by Daniel Berrigan and Robert Coles; Updated introduction and afterword by the authors* 6 x 9, 224 pp, Quality PB, ISBN 1-893361-40-3 **$16.95**

God Lives in Glass: Reflections of God for Adults through the Eyes of Children
by Robert J. Landy, PhD; Foreword by Sandy Eisenberg Sasso
7 x 6, 64 pp, HC, Full-color illus., ISBN 1-893361-30-6 **$12.95**

God Within: Our Spiritual Future—As Told by Today's New Adults *Edited by Jon M. Sweeney and the Editors at SkyLight Paths* 6 x 9, 176 pp, Quality PB, ISBN 1-893361-15-2 **$14.95**

Jewish Spirituality: A Brief Introduction for Christians *by Lawrence Kushner*
5½ x 8½, 112 pp, Quality PB, ISBN 1-58023-150-0 **$12.95** *(a Jewish Lights book)*

A Jewish Understanding of the New Testament
by Rabbi Samuel Sandmel; New preface by Rabbi David Sandmel
5½ x 8½, 384 pp, Quality PB, ISBN 1-59473-048-2 **$19.99**

Journeys of Simplicity: Traveling Light with Thomas Merton, Basho, Edward Abbey, Annie Dillard & Others *by Philip Harnden* 5 x 7¼, 128 pp, HC, ISBN 1-893361-76-4 **$16.95**

Keeping Spiritual Balance As We Grow Older: More than 65 Creative Ways to Use Purpose, Prayer, and the Power of Spirit to Build a Meaningful Retirement
by Molly and Bernie Srode 8 x 8, 224 pp, Quality PB, ISBN 1-59473-042-3 **$16.99**

The Monks of Mount Athos: A Western Monk's Extraordinary Spiritual Journey on Eastern Holy Ground *by M. Basil Pennington, ocso; Foreword by Archimandrite Dionysios*
6 x 9, 256 pp, 10+ b/w line drawings, Quality PB, ISBN 1-893361-78-0 **$18.95**

One God Clapping: The Spiritual Path of a Zen Rabbi *by Alan Lew with Sherrill Jaffe*
5½ x 8½, 336 pp, Quality PB, ISBN 1-58023-115-2 **$16.95** *(a Jewish Lights book)*

Spiritual Practice

Divining the Body
Reclaim the Holiness of Your Physical Self *by Jan Phillips*
A practical and inspiring guidebook for connecting the body and soul in spiritual practice. Leads you into a milieu of reverence, mystery, and delight, helping you discover a redeemed sense of self.
8 x 8, 256 pp, Quality PB, ISBN 1-59473-080-6 **$16.99**

Finding Time for the Timeless
Spirituality in the Workweek *by John McQuiston II*
Simple, refreshing stories that provide you with examples of how you can refocus and enrich your daily life using prayer or meditation, ritual, and other forms of spiritual practice. 5½ x 6½, 208 pp, HC, ISBN 1-59473-035-0 **$17.99**

The Gospel of Thomas: A Guidebook for Spiritual Practice
by Ron Miller; Translations by Stevan Davies
An innovative guide to bring a new spiritual classic into daily life. Offers a way to translate the wisdom of the Gospel of Thomas into daily practice, manifesting in your life the same consciousness revealed in Jesus of Nazareth. Written for readers of all religious backgrounds, this guidebook will help you to apply Jesus's wisdom to your own life and to the world around you.
6 x 9, 160 pp, Quality PB, ISBN 1-59473-047-4 **$14.99**

The Knitting Way: A Guide to Spiritual Self-Discovery
by Linda Skolnik and Janice MacDaniels
Through sharing stories, hands-on explorations, and daily cultivation, Skolnik and MacDaniels help you see beyond the surface of a simple craft in order to discover ways in which nuances of knitting can apply to the larger scheme of life and spirituality. Includes original knitting patterns.
7 x 9, 240 pp, Quality PB, ISBN 1-59473-079-2 **$16.99**

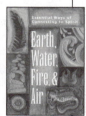

Earth, Water, Fire, and Air: Essential Ways of Connecting to Spirit
by Cait Johnson 6 x 9, 224 pp, HC, ISBN 1-893361-65-9 **$19.95**

Forty Days to Begin a Spiritual Life
Today's Most Inspiring Teachers Help You on Your Way
Edited by Maura Shaw and the Editors at SkyLight Paths; Foreword by Dan Wakefield
7 x 9, 144 pp, Quality PB, ISBN 1-893361-48-9 **$16.95**

Labyrinths from the Outside In
Walking to Spiritual Insight—A Beginner's Guide
by Donna Schaper and Carole Ann Camp
6 x 9, 208 pp, b/w illus. and photographs, Quality PB, ISBN 1-893361-18-7 **$16.95**

Practicing the Sacred Art of Listening: A Guide to Enrich Your Relationships and Kindle Your Spiritual Life—The Listening Center Workshop
by Kay Lindahl 8 x 8, 176 pp, Quality PB, ISBN 1-893361-85-3 **$16.95**

The Sacred Art of Bowing: Preparing to Practice
by Andi Young 5½ x 8½, 128 pp, b/w illus., Quality PB, ISBN 1-893361-82-9 **$14.95**

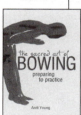

The Sacred Art of Chant: Preparing to Practice
by Ana Hernandez 5½ x 8½, 192 pp, Quality PB, ISBN 1-59473-036-9 **$15.99**

The Sacred Art of Fasting: Preparing to Practice
by Thomas Ryan, CSP 5½ x 8½, 192 pp, Quality PB, ISBN 1-59473-078-4 **$15.99**

The Sacred Art of Listening: Forty Reflections for Cultivating a Spiritual Practice
by Kay Lindahl; Illustrations by Amy Schnapper
8 x 8, 160 pp, Illus., Quality PB, ISBN 1-893361-44-6 **$16.99**

Sacred Speech: A Practical Guide for Keeping Spirit in Your Speech
by Rev. Donna Schaper 6 x 9, 176 pp, Quality PB, ISBN 1-59473-068-7 **$15.99**;
HC, ISBN 1-893361-74-8 **$21.95**

AVAILABLE FROM BETTER BOOKSTORES.
TRY YOUR BOOKSTORE FIRST.

About SKYLIGHT PATHS Publishing

SkyLight Paths Publishing is creating a place where people of different spiritual traditions come together for challenge and inspiration, a place where we can help each other understand the mystery that lies at the heart of our existence.

Through spirituality, our religious beliefs are increasingly becoming a part of our lives—rather than *apart* from our lives. While many of us may be more interested than ever in spiritual growth, we may be less firmly planted in traditional religion. Yet, we do want to deepen our relationship to the sacred, to learn from our own as well as from other faith traditions, and to practice in new ways.

SkyLight Paths sees both believers and seekers as a community that increasingly transcends traditional boundaries of religion and denomination—people wanting to learn from each other, *walking together, finding the way.*

For your information and convenience, at the back of this book we have provided a list of other SkyLight Paths books you might find interesting and useful. They cover the following subjects:

Buddhism / Zen	Gnosticism	Mysticism
Catholicism	Hinduism /	Poetry
Children's Books	Vedanta	Prayer
Christianity	Inspiration	Religious Etiquette
Comparative	Islam / Sufism	Retirement
Religion	Judaism / Kabbalah /	Spiritual Biography
Current Events	Enneagram	Spiritual Direction
Earth-Based	Meditation	Spirituality
Spirituality	Midrash Fiction	Women's Interest
Global Spiritual	Monasticism	Worship
Perspectives		

Or phone, fax, mail or e-mail to: SKYLIGHT PATHS Publishing
Sunset Farm Offices, Route 4 • P.O. Box 237 • Woodstock, Vermont 05091
Tel: (802) 457-4000 • Fax: (802) 457-4004 • www.skylightpaths.com
Credit card orders: (800) 962-4544 (8:30AM–5:30PM ET Monday–Friday)
Generous discounts on quantity orders. SATISFACTION GUARANTEED. Prices subject to change.

For more information about each book,
visit our website at www.skylightpaths.com